A Love Sublime

By

Teresa Banks

A Love Sublime
ISBN 978-1-7373694-8-6   Softbound
ISBN 979-8-9859076-9-8   Hardbound
ISBN 979-8-9861485-3-3   EBook
Copyright © 2022 TE Banks

Request for information should be addressed to:
Curry Brothers Marketing and Publishing Group
P.O. Box 247 Haymarket, VA 20168

All rights reserved. No part of this publication may be reproduced, stored in a retrieval system, or transmitted in any form or by any means, electronic, mechanical, photocopy, recording, or any other, except for brief quotations in printed reviews, without the prior permission of the publisher.

Executive Editing by Joniece Jackson
Cover Design by Alex Cotton (*Unrelenting Media*)
Manuscript Formatting by Joniece Jackson

This book is dedicated to
My daughter Catina and grandson Nicholas

Special dedication to Ivy
Forever in my Heart

Blessings and Light

Acknowledgments

I want to acknowledge the people who were there from the beginning. They gave me encouragement to finish my "Love Story."

First, God, he watched over me and helped me move forward. He let me know, it was time.

Blessings to The Curry Brothers and their team, I feel blessed to have these men and women in my life.

Jeffery, my attorney and friend. When I stopped writing he understood, he said, "You love your characters, you don't want your relationship with them to end." He was right, once I was able to give my ancestors a loving end, the words flowed.

Josie, she encouraged me with gentle persuasion to write something every day. She became my "Little Sister."

Special Acknowledgment to Linda, Kim and Buddy, who helped me through some of my darkest days.

Prelude

Black Women and Black Men have been sexualized, using sex as a weapon. Sex has been used to barter, for leverage. Sex has been used for basic human needs of food and water, instead of the expression of love. Sexual impulse is an emotional roller coaster that drains positive strength and energy.

My female ancestors used their sexual energy to endure, love, and elevate. I honor these phenomenal women and their stories. I write from my heart, so they will never be forgotten. Women who, with the help of God, triumphed, overcoming obstacles. Women who loved deeply and without hesitation to bring forth the next generation.

Chapter 1

My maternal grandmother, Jewel Johnson, was born June 1, 1915, on a farm in Indianapolis, Indiana. No doctor or midwife; no indoor plumbing; no electricity. Jewel's mother left her at 6 weeks old to be raised by her maternal grandmother, Lizzie, who was strict and cruel. The farmhouse was heated with a potbelly stove. As Jewel became older, she had to pump water from a well, the outhouse would freeze in the winter. It was a hard life, but this was the only life my grandmother and Jewel knew. Jewel could not understand why Grandmother Lizzie was so mean to her. She was obedient, worked hard doing her chores, and sang the loudest in church. As time passed, Jewel accepted her life and her treatment from an unhappy and temperamental 70-year-old woman.

    As Jewel grew older, her education took a back seat to work the farm. However, Grandmother Lizzie only allowed Jewel to complete the fourth grade. Education was never a priority for little Black children who lived on farms on the outskirts of town. Jewel was only able to read, write her name, add, and subtract when she was forced to leave school at the age of nine. When Jewel was 13, on a warm spring day in April of 1928, while feeding the livestock, she was summoned to the house. Her heart was beating so hard she thought she may have a heart attack. Grandmother Lizzie never called Jewel to the house unless it was sundown and time for dinner.

    As she ran into the kitchen, through the afternoon haze, there stood this beautiful woman. It was her mother, Ida. Ida was a shapely woman with light-brown skin, coal-black hair, and gray eyes. She wore a hat with a peacock feather. Around her shoulders she wore fox fur; the mouth of the fox clamped down on its own feet. Her suit was green and hugged her curves perfectly. There was something about the reunion that disturbed Jewel. She didn't know what was wrong, she just had a funny feeling. In the kitchen, while looking at her mother and grandmother, she realized she was the darkest person in the room. She did not have that redbone color. Was this the reason Grandmother Lizzie was so mean to her? Was this the reason her mother left her as an infant? Jewel felt self-conscience at that moment; she knew she was different. Mother Ida explained that she had been traveling to different cities where she thought she could make a better impression and find a husband without the cumbersome ties of a child. She decided to settle in Allen, Tennessee where she married the local doctor. Mother Ida was now married to a doctor, they had no children, but he wanted a family. Today, she had returned to the farm to take Jewel with her, not as a daughter but, as her niece and companion. She further explained that to make her husband happy, she told him her sister and brother-in-law had died from a fever and their daughter, her niece Jewel, needed a home. He thought this was such a blessing; he was going to have a daughter. Jewel was to pretend to be her niece and her husband could never know the truth.

Without another word, Jewel found herself packed, scrubbed clean, hair put up into two large braids, and wearing a dress that was bought for her train ride. Jewel said goodbye to Grandmother Lizzie who gave her a half-hearted hug. Mother Ida and Jewel walked down the dusty road for a ride to the train station. Jewel realized she would never return to the farm or see Grandmother Lizzie again. Instead of being sad, she looked forward to leaving the farm and having her first train ride, she was happy. Mother Ida explained more to Jewel as the train clicked and rocked through the night.

"I am sorry for leaving you and running away from my responsibility as a mother. I married Doctor Ira Jones seven years ago. I am unable to have more children. Dr. Ira, my husband, wants to be a father which is why I told him the story of my sister dying. I told him I wanted to take my sister's daughter to raise. He agreed that I should bring my niece into our home," she said. "I came back to the farm for you. This was the best way to bring you back into my life and make up for the past thirteen years; I will be your aunt and Dr. Ira will be a wonderful father."

Jewel was taught in church that to lie was a sin, but she didn't want to disobey her mother, so she prayed, asked for forgiveness, and decided to obey and honor her mother. She would now be called, Aunt Ida. Jewel looked forward to her new life in Allen, TN but also felt anxious and afraid. She was afraid for her mother's soul because she was telling two lies that they both had to live with. First, Mother Ida had no sister, and second, Jewel was her daughter, not her niece. How could she lie to a man she took vows with before God and put her innocent daughter in the middle of all this?

After an exhausting eight-hour trip, Aunt Ida and Jewel arrived in the small town of Allen, TN; population two thousand. Aunt Ida told her the history of this small town. "Allen was settled by freed slaves and was busy growing strong and expanding."

Jewel thought the town looked so shiny and new. There were no dirt roads, the streets were paved with streetlights and sidewalks. They traveled to her new home on Ruth Street. Everyone waved and spoke to Mrs. Jones; she was the wife of the town's only doctor; he was loved and respected. The feelings were also relayed to Aunt Ida. Passing the Church of the Holy Spirit, it was painted bright white with large white columns holding up the roof that was painted the most beautiful shade of blue Jewel had ever seen. It made her imagine angels sitting there watching over the town. The bells started to ring in the steeple as it was noon. Jewel closed her eyes and pretended the bells were ringing just for her. Jewel started to sing a sweet song of love to God and his Son she had learned from Grandmother Lizzie. Aunt Ida remembered the song, she looked at Jewel and smiled as a tear rolled down her cheek.

The home of Dr. Ira and Mrs. Jones was a grand two-story stone house that looked like a mansion lived in by rich white families in the city of Indianapolis. There was a large porch that wrapped around the entire front and sides of the house. Large hanging ferns swung in the breeze with rows upon rows of rose bushes in front of the porch with tulips lining both sides of the walkway to this grand house. Seven large white stone steps led up to the porch, which was painted a deep rich brown. Jewel thought she would disappear in its darkness. The ceiling of the porch was painted the same blue as the church, with fluffy white clouds. The house was painted a bright yellow, trimmed in white. The windows reflected the afternoon sun like sparkling stars. The front door was wide with glass that was etched with flowers and leaves. When the door opened; Jewel could not believe how beautiful it was. She had never seen a house like this. On the first floor, there was a sitting room with a dark-green sofa and gold throw pillows, three overstuffed chairs, tables with lamps that had the invention of electric light bulbs. Jewel thought this light came from angels it was so soft; it gave her dark skin a warm glow. There were drapes of gold, trimmed in the same dark green as the sofa and chairs. The walls were painted a clean white. Through the sitting room was the dining room. It was grand with a large table and eight chairs with gold cushions and a large centerpiece of fresh flowers. A bay window with lace curtains allowed the afternoon light to flood the room. The next room was the kitchen. A large stove stood next to the cabinets with countertops that connected to a large hearth for baking. The cook was baking cakes for dinner; the room smelled wonderful. There was a small table next to the window and back door; Jewel was told this was for the cook and the cleaner to take their meals. Dr. Ira did not want the help to live in because he wanted the ladies to be home with their families in the evening. The cook Sadie, and the cleaner Mary, would come to the house at 6 a.m. and leave at 3 p.m., they would be asked to stay later for parties. The backyard was full of flowers and an herb garden. Jewel was excited to see there were no animals to care for.

Aunt Ida explained, "The Town Square has a general store, the farmers come to the square three times a week with fresh meats, vegetables, and dairy foods. I never liked the farm, I'm happy Sadie shops for our food. Dr. Ira is a country doctor, but I refused to marry him unless he moved to a town where I could live in a house with conveniences of the time. He was so in love with me he agreed, but his heart still longed for the country and farm life.

The Jones family still has their farm outside of Allen where his five brothers, two sisters, and his mother live. His father passed away before he finished medical school. That fact always made Dr. Ira sad because his father worked the farm and two jobs in town to keep him in medical school, but he did not live to see him graduate. He felt guilty especially when he got married, moved from the farm to a house in town."

Dr. Ira and Aunt Ida's bedroom was the first room at the top-right of the stairs. It was a large room with a huge four-poster bed, a veranda opening onto the back garden. Jewel could not believe how large the room was; it was as large as the entire kitchen and front room at Grandmother Lizzie's farmhouse. Further down the hall was another bedroom set up as Dr. Ira's office, it was filled with books, and his diploma hung on the wall. In front of a large window was an oversized desk draped in dark red material with pictures of his family and all the babies he had delivered. Their wedding picture sat on his desk; Jewel was certain she saw sadness in his eyes. The next room was the bathroom. Again, Jewel was so excited she couldn't hold it in, she started to sing. The bathroom was painted a bright yellow, with a white sink, a large white tub with gold claw feet, and to her amazement, a toilet. She had never seen a toilet in her thirteen years of life. Jewel was amazed at the way it flushed everything away, no more outhouse! The final room at the end of the hall on the left was to be her room. She opened the door to a glare coming from the window but when her eyes came into focus, she knew she had been blessed. The room was painted a pale rose pink with white lace curtains at the window. There was a dresser with a mirror and sitting on top were combs, brushes, and lilac water. A tall closet was on the far wall with dresses and shoes;

Jewel started to weep for joy because she never had a dress before and now, she had five! She also had two new pairs of shoes. When she lived on the farm, she only had hand-me-down shoes from the church. She fell backward on the bed and dangled her feet. It was a feather bed, incredibly soft with two big pillows and fluffy blankets. The bed was a perfect size for one; no longer did she have a pallet on the floor in front of the kitchen fire.

Chapter 2

Jewel woke to the crow of a neighbor's rooster. It was a warm Saturday morning; the birds were singing, and she could smell the honeysuckle bushes outside her bedroom window. Today was special, it was June 1, 1931, and she was turning sixteen. Jewel was going to have her very first birthday party! She had been a dutiful "niece" over the past three years. Dr. Ira had insisted Jewel return to school and finish her primary education. Jewel was able to attend school and graduate from the ninth grade. She enjoyed school but it wasn't enough to keep her interest. She knew she would never advance to college; book learning was just too hard.

She enjoyed learning how to manage a household with Ms. Sadie. Jewel learned to pick the best meats and vegetables at the market, she also learned to balance the kitchen budget in a weekly bank balance book. Ms. Sadie taught Jewel how to season meats for cooking and how to preserve them for storage through the winter. She taught her how-to put-up vegetables and fruit preserves. No one in Allen could bake better biscuits, cakes, or pies. These lessons she learned with no problem, she thought working with her hands would please the Lord more than book learning. Ms. Mary, the housekeeper, taught her how to clean the house, do laundry, make beds, and keep the house dust and dirt free. Occasionally Mary would bring her two-year-old daughter to work and those were days Jewel enjoyed the most, she loved babies. Mary noticed this and remarked to Ms. Sadie, "Jewel will make a wonderful mother someday."

Jewel bathed and braided her shiny black hair into a single long braid and wrapped it around her head like a crown. She picked out a crisp pink dress to start the day. As she looked in the mirror, she could see the curves of a woman; she had gotten them from Aunt Ida. She smiled because she was looking more like her every day, except with darker skin. She thought, 'I have her coal-black naturally curly hair with soft waves and her gray eyes. When people remarked to Aunt Ida how much she looked like her "natural daughter" she would laugh and say, "All the women in my family look alike." Aunt Ida would tell everyone Jewel was the odd-one-out in the family, referring to her dark skin. The words hurt Jewel. Having her mother deny her and talk about the darkness of her skin color, she was her only child. This made Jewel sad, tears welled up in her eyes, but because Aunt Ida was her mother, she would continue to honor "the lie."

As Jewel ran down the steps to the dining room for breakfast, she could smell the coffee and the wonderful fragrance from the oven, Ms. Sadie was baking her birthday cake for the party. Dr. Ira was sitting at the table drinking his coffee and reading the paper, he looked tired. He had delivered twins the night before and had just only gotten home in the early morning. When he heard Jewel come into the dining room he put the paper down, placed his cup on the saucer, and asked for his morning hug. Dr. Ira treated Jewel like she was his natural daughter, not an orphan that had been taken in on charity. Jewel called him Father. He was a tall man with a slim build, large strong hands, and a warm smile that always made Jewel feel safe. He had salt and pepper hair cut close with a right-side part, a sharp thin mustache, also noticeably light skin. He never made Jewel feel bad about her dark skin.

Dr. Ira always told her she was beautiful. He would say, "Jewel, God made you and you are perfect in his eyes. The darkest berries on the vines are the sweetest, the dark red apples are the best ones to eat, and the wine Jesus blessed at the Last Supper, was strong with a dark red color. Your Aunt Ida is color struck like many in our community. I want you to be a proud woman. Don't let the color of your skin make you feel any less than a child of God, he loves you and so do I."

He then asked Jewel to tell him the plans for the birthday party. Jewel sat at the dining room table with Father and started to tell him about the party.

"I did not have any input about the party plans. Aunt Ida planned the menu, decorated the house, and she only invited children from the best families in Allen." Jewel continued, "Aunt Ida has worked so hard on my party. I don't want to seem ungrateful, but I would have liked to help." Father smiled and said, "I know how your aunt loves to plan parties so I'm sure it will be a wonderful affair."

Aunt Ida did not invite any of Jewel's friends from church, she only went to church on Easter and Christmas. She thought the ladies in the church wanted her husband and her life, so she did not associate with them, or their children. She was only polite when they came to the house for medical attention. Father took Jewel to church every Sunday. They arrived early for Sunday school, stayed for the sermon, and stayed for fellowship dinner after service. Aunt Ida hated Sundays and the time they spent together. Jewel sensed she might be jealous of the time they spent together and that her husband was acting like a true parent. She would complain and have a hissy fit every Sunday. Father would just listen, nod his head, and then retreat to his office. After he would leave the room, Aunt Ida would go into Jewel's room in a rage, sometimes taking a strap to her, saying how much of a plague she was and that she regretted ever getting her from the farm. Jewel believed at times that Aunt Ida hated her, but she loved her mother. She did not understand why God would give her this burden. She thought this was a test and prayed every day for strength to be an obedient child.

The party was to start at 5 p.m. in the garden, at 7 p.m. dinner would be served followed by cake and punch. Aunt Ida invited the parents along with the boys and girls. She made it clear to Jewel this was a special night for "her" to show the self-assertive women, husbands, and their spoiled children she was just as good, or better than they were. Aunt Ida told Jewel to be on her best behavior. She told her if she didn't make a good impression or embarrassed her, she would take the strap to her and make Father send her away. Jewel did not know how she wanted her to act. She was scared and in tears, as she sat on the side of the bed, staring at her party dress.

As 5 p.m. approached, Jewel became more upset, and her tears flowed. Aunt Ida had taken all the joy out of her day. It was no longer the joyful day she woke up to. She looked at her party dress; it was white with little yellow flowers around the neck and a yellow sash around her waist. She had yellow ribbons in her hair and yellow ribbons laced her shoes. The more she looked at the dress, the more she cried, she dropped to her knees to pray.

"Lord please take this fear away. Make me strong and true tonight. Thank you for my 16 years of life. These blessings I ask in your name. Amen."

After her prayer, there was a knock at her door, it was Father, she let him in. "Daughter, are you ready for your party?"

"Father, I am so afraid I will embarrass you and Aunt Ida tonight with my country ways."

Father smiled and said, "You could never embarrass me or my house. I could not have asked for a better daughter. You may not be my blood, but you are my child, I love you. I will love you even from my grave."

With those words, her strength was renewed by God's grace through her Father. She was ready to dress, face Aunt Ida, and greet her party guests.

Chapter 3

Jewel dressed in her party dress and adjusted her "crown." She brushed her hair and added honeysuckle blossoms, she splashed on the lilac water. As she looked at herself in the full-length mirror, her mind started to drift back to the farm and stories Grandmother Lizzie told her as a small child.

"Our original ancestry dates to the 1700s in South Africa. Your great-great-grandfather was a prince of his tribe. One morning he went alone to hunt in the bush and was captured by slavers from the territory of Louisiana. He was taken by ship to the Port of New Orleans. From there he was taken to the St. Louis Hotel where he was examined from head-to-toe with his description written in the Registry of Slaves. This registry was kept for 2 reasons. The first was for the plantation owner to know which slaves he had bought and the second was if the slave ran away the Negro Hunters would know who and what to look for, especially if the slave was marked or maimed. He was given a new name, Fontain, and his description was recorded as follows:

> Male from South Africa. Approximate age, 22. 6 ft tall, no disease, good teeth. Large, well-formed genitals, look good for breeding. Strong back, able to lift, can also work in the field. Value, $100.00.

He was sold to the Lucien Plantation to work in the sugarcane fields. He was dropped in the slave quarters to start his life, not as a member of the royal family of his tribe, but as a slave stripped of all dignity and title. The elder slave in his quarters was Benjamin, he had been on the Lucien plantation for 65 years, he was born there he knew the white family and his taskmasters well.

He warned Fontain, "Learn English, do not speak your native language, do not make eye contact with the white family or any white man on the place, and never look at any of the white women no matter what is said or done. Heed my warning it will save you from beatings or worse.

Go about your day, harvest the sugarcane and accept your fate because no one from Africa will ever see you again and no one is going to come to your rescue."

Fontain replied "I am a prince I do not believe what you are telling me. I am the son of a king, I am sure I will be able to explain this to the whites, my confinement is a mistake."

That was an awful mistake for Fontain to try and reason with the taskmaster, John. In his best English Fontain said, "I am a prince and I demand to see the plantation owner."

John looked at Fontain, smiled, and said, "Tell me, Prince, how can I help you?"

"I should not be here I was taken against my will!!"

"Boy, you belong to the Lucien family! Get back to your cabin before I beat the black off you."

Fontain would not back down, "I need to speak with the owner, not a hired hand."

John turned, his face red with anger, and said, "You don't know who I am, but I'm gonna show you."

Fontain was beaten and hung upside down by his feet from a tree in the slave quarters with no food and water for three days.

Benjamin saw Master Lucien and asked, "Please Sir, can I cut down Fontain? He will die if he hangs any longer and if he dies, you will lose your money."

He knew the Lucien family never lost money on slaves.

"You're a smart boy," Master Lucien told Benjamin. "Cut him down, get him fixed up, and return him to the field."

"Thank you, Master Lucien. I will take care of him."

Fontain was cut down; he was near death. He now understood what Benjamin had warned, his fate was sealed. To survive he would have to submit to the will of the white plantation owners, their words were law. Fountain's dark ebony skin was ashen from lack of water. He was given a week to heal from his wounds before he returned to the sugarcane fields. Because of his weakened condition, a female slave by the name of Patience was sent to his cabin to help him recover. Patience had also been born on the Lucien Plantation, she and her mother worked in the big house.

When Master Dupree's wife and child died during childbirth, he went mad with grief. He did not want to be alone in the house, he would walk the plantation at all hours of the night. He would curse, scream, and run through the swamp. He would be gone for days. Master Dupree had gone to the swamp on a sweltering summer night; he was bitten by mosquitoes and came down with a fever. While he lay near death on the swamp banks, Marie, a young Creole girl living in the swamp saw him. She decided to help Master Dupree and took him back to her hut. Marie had lived in the swamp for 10 years; she knew what plants and mud could be used as medicine. The plantation where she was born had burned down and her mother fled to the swamp; they were never found by the Negro Hunters. Her mother passed away and to remain free, she continued to live in the swamp alone, in peace, she was 19 years old. Master Dupree was in a bad way, his spirit and will to live left him when his wife and baby girl died. It had been 2 years, but he was like a man possessed.

His brother Abe was running the plantation, in hopes that his brother would recover. Marie knew none of this, but she was a kind girl and could not stand to see anyone or anything suffer. She started to nurse Master Dupree back to health. His body had fits and convulsions for three long weeks, but the fever finally broke. He opened his eyes and saw Marie for the very first time with clear eyes. She was beautiful. A sweet smile with skin the color of spring wheat. She had long straight hair the color of amber and eyes like a bright blue sky. Her mother told her she was the plantation owner's daughter. Master Conte loved her like a wife and treated her well. His barren wife found out about Marie and burned the place to the ground. Master Conte, her father, was killed trying to protect them, so her mother took Marie and fled to the safety of the swamp.

Master Dupree recovered, there was an instant attraction between Marie and Master Dupree. She was lonely, and he was finally at peace about the loss of his wife and child. When he was strong enough to travel, they returned to the Lucien Plantation where Marie was installed as his companion and lover. With her arrival, the torture and daily whippings stopped. Master Dupree was kind and happy, his brother Abe was sent back to Mississippi, there was a feeling of relief and joy amongst the slaves because he was a harsh supervisor, cruel and twisted. Over the next 20 years, Marie bore five children for Master Dupree, all girls. Patience was the oldest and looked just like her mother. She was beautiful, had long black hair, a peaches and cream complexion with gray eyes.

Fontain began to respond to the herbs Patience used to bring him back to life. He was able to walk in a few days. After a week had passed Fontain was able to eat and keep his food down. Once he returned to the sugarcane field, Patience would bring him a drink at the end of the day, which made him stronger. Just as her mother had healed Master Dupree's mind, body, and spirit, her daughter Patience was doing the same for Fontain.

One evening as Fontain drank his special drink, he said to Patience, "I love you."

Patience smiled and said, "I love you too."

They fell into each other arms and made love. Afterward, he told Patience, "I want to take you as my wife."

"I want to be your wife."

She walked on air as she returned to her mother's quarters.

"Mother, I have fallen in love with Fontain. He told me tonight he also loves me, and he wants to take me as his wife."

"I'm so happy you have found a man to love and who loves you. Your union will be wonderful. Fontain is the same as you and I prayed that you would not experience the heartbreak of loving a man you can never claim as your own."

Marie wanted her children to have a normal life and not be slaves. She would make sure this would happen with all her children, starting with Patience. She knew Master Dupree loved their children; he made a promise that he'd never sell their children. Marie wanted her girls to be free. Master Dupree agreed to the union. He was happy that his firstborn had found love. He admired Fountain, his spirit, and his bloodline, but would never be able to say that to anyone, not even Marie. The union was in the garden of the big house and was attended by all the slaves, her mother, and her four sisters Lilly (10), Rose (12), Angel (15), and Autumn (17). It was a grand affair, in terms of slave unions. Master Dupree stood on the second-floor veranda watching with the pride of a real father. There was a fiddle-player, cakes, hams, turkeys, and all kinds of vegetables. The stores of the plantation were opened for the union. Marie gave the blessing and joined her daughter with Fontain.

The party was going well into the night when Fontain whispered into Patience's ear, "Come with me to our new quarters. Let the others enjoy the food and freedom for the night."

She smiled, took his hand, and they ran toward their new home. It was a beautiful night. It was more than they could have ever imagined. They fell into each other's arms and made love through the night falling asleep with sweet dreams of a family and freedom. After the wedding, Fontain returned to the fields with a light heart as he planned his future and freedom with his wife.

Marie was able to freely travel to town. One day she heard of the "Underground Railroad" she knew this was her chance to get her children to freedom. She knew Fontain kept the flame burning for freedom and now that he was married, it burned hotter than ever. She got money from Master Dupree for her daughters and son-in-law. On the next full moon, they would be able to join other slaves on their trip North. They packed food and water for the trip, all was kept secret because she did not want to alert the other slaves to her plan and risk something going wrong. On

October 30, 1810, during the harvest moon, Fontain, Patience, and her four sisters joined the Underground Railroad for their trip North. They all said goodbye to Marie and Master Dupree, and he hugged his daughter's farewell. The trip proved to be much more difficult than anyone had expected. A sudden rainstorm caused the tunnels to flood and Patience's little sisters, Lilly and Rose, were swept away and drowned. Their destination was to be Baltimore, Maryland but with her sisters dead, Patience lost the will to continue. Fontain decided to stop and leave the Underground Railroad in Ohio.

They were on their own, but Patience seemed to feel better with the sunshine on her face. Fontain and his family came upon a Native American village on the banks of the Allegheny River. They were greeted by Chief White Horse. The Indigenous people helped Fontain set up a shelter for him and his family. Fontain told Chief White Horse the story of how he was captured and his time as a slave. The Chief knew all too well of the slavers from the south as he had people from his tribe taken away. Fontain made an agreement with Chief White Horse for five acres of land in exchange for his sister-in-law Autumn to be united with his son. Autumn agreed because she had fallen deeply in love with Flying Eagle and wanted to start a life with him. They were united and Fontain got his five acres.

Fontain, Patience, and Angel built a log cabin and farmed their land. They raised cows, chickens, horses, and other livestock. Fontain traded with the French Trappers and his extended family, the Native Americans. All was well until trade relations and wars started between the Native Americans and whites, who wanted to claim their land with help from Union Soldiers. Fontain and his family were driven from their land, they went to Indiana, where they settled on a small farm outside Indianapolis. The slave's name of Lucien from the plantation was changed to Johnson. On the farm, the family prospered buying more land and building a sturdy home for all to enjoy."

Grandmother Lizzie was born in this farmhouse, she was the only child of Marie and Fontain Johnson. Ida and Jewel were also born on this land in Indiana, in this little farmhouse. Fontain and Marie lived together on their farm all their lives. Fontain died at eighty years old, and Marie died the following year. Aunt Angel never married or had children, she lived to be 90. They were all buried on the property. Grandmother Lizzie was an only child. Mother Ida was also an only child, as was Jewel. Jewel thought of her ancestry and was proud; her great-great-grandfather was a King and her great-grandfather, was a Prince of Africa.

She held her head high, walked down in a slow, regal manner, and greeted her guests like royalty.

Chapter 4

Jewel walked down the staircase with a pride and elegance she had never known before, and it showed to her guests. Everyone commented how beautiful she was, all wishing her a happy 16th birthday. Jewel had her first waltz with Father, afterwards, the party was in full swing. She danced, sang, and talked with the parents of some of the most prominent families in Allen.

Aunt Ida was surprised at the ease with which Jewel talked and interacted with the most educated adults in the room, and she was jealous. This party was for her to shine and be the belle of the ball, not Jewel. When she tried to inject herself into conversations, the women would turn away while the husbands would clear their throats. The more Aunt Ida was rebuffed, the madder and out of control, she became. She started to drink Father's bourbon whisky, slurring her words, and stumbling about the room, which made everyone even more distant. Father was uncomfortable and embarrassed by her behavior. He took her away to the butler's pantry to sit and compose herself before dinner.

While Father and Aunt Ida were out of the room, Jewel became the hostess and focus of the party. She felt beautiful, like the lady of the house. The sun started to set, and the party guests started to move into the dining room for dinner when the doorbell rang, it was the Cotton Family, the wealthiest and most respected family in town. Mr. Cotton, his wife Aurora, and their handsome son Victor had arrived; the crowd started to buzz and greet them as they entered the house.

The Cottons helped settle Allen, Tennessee. Mr. George Douglas, Cotton Jr's father, was a plantation owner in Louisiana. His boyhood friend was John Carter, his parents owned the adjoining plantation, Willow Oaks. They attended the same college and graduated together. When Mr. Cotton returned home, he went to dinner at Willow Oaks and met their house slave, Aurora. She was the daughter of house slave Kitty; her father was Master John Carter. When a wife passed away, it was tradition for the master of the plantation to take up with a female house slave. Master Lee had four daughters with Kitty, Aurora was 17 years old and his firstborn. He had no children with his deceased wife.

When Aurora finished her chores, she had the run of the house. She would boss the other house slaves, no one ever talked back or complained. Her mother Kitty didn't work in the house, she was Master

John's constant companion. She served him and was at his beck and call. Aurora looked like Master John and there was no doubt that she was his daughter. She had his curly black hair, his green eyes, and a beautiful caramel completion. She was shapely with an ample bosom and a smile that could light up a room.

When George Cotton Jr. saw her for the first time, he was struck dumb, he knew he had to have her. After dinner he talked with Master Lee; he wanted to purchase Aurora and have her as his companion at his family's plantation. He offered $1,000.00. He was a greedy man and accepted the offer. The money overrode the fact that he was selling his own daughter.

"Kitty, I am selling Aurora to George Cotton. They will be leaving first thing in the morning," Master Lee explained.

"How can you sell one of your children?! You told me you would never sell our babies," Kitty screamed. She ran to the pantry, got a knife, and stabbed him in the chest. "I will cut your heart out for selling my baby!" Kitty continued to scream.

The cook and butler pulled her off Master Lee as she stabbed him in the chest. The wound was not fatal, but it scarred him enough to sell Kitty and her 3 daughters to a plantation in Mississippi; they were never seen again.

"That bastard is going to sell your sisters and me at the slave market in town tomorrow. I want you to know we love you and you will always be in my heart. I am so sorry I brought you into this world. This is not a good time, or place, to be a woman. Go with your new Master, keep God in your heart, and pray you never have to suffer the pain of losing your babies," Kitty said as tears streamed down her face,

"I will never submit to this man," Aurora cried. "He has ruined our family…I love you. I will always remember you and my sisters."

She arrived at her new home, fully aware of what her father had done to her and her family. She decided she would never submit to George Cotton and would fight him every chance she got. The first night he called her to his bed, she fought him; scratched his face, kicked, and screamed. He did not want to take her by force, he had fallen in love with her and wanted her love in return.

This went on for two weeks and George's patience was wearing thin. He decided to have her moved to the slave quarters and have her work in the field.

Aurora had never worked in the sugar cane fields. The harsh working and living conditions took their toll on her, she lost weight, her hair started to fall out, and her skin was sun and wind burned. Her hands were no longer soft, her smile was gone, and her green eyes started to dim. Mr. Cotton saw Aurora was proud and would not ask to return to the house. When the rainy season started, there was a flood in the slave quarters; several huts were washed away. Twenty-five slaves drowned and 35 were missing. Mr. Cotton looked for Aurora in the middle of the rainstorm and found her clinging to life, holding onto a tree limb in the raging water. He jumped into the water, started swimming, and grabbed her just as the tree limb washed away. She was exhausted and fainted in his arms. Looking at her, broke his heart, Mr. Cotton never believed in slavery and tried to protect his slaves as much as possible, but he knew if he wanted a normal life with Aurora, he would need to leave the plantation and Louisiana.

"Aurora will only get worse if we stay here, she will die. I love her and the only way we can have a normal life together is if I take her North where she can pass for white, and we can be married," said Jr.

"I understand you want this woman, but what about your obligation to your family and the plantation? You will throw all that away for a slave?" Cotton Sr. asked.

"Yes, I will. She is more than a slave to me. She is the woman I love and want to marry. I want to have children with her."

His father, George Sr., was completely against the idea of his son going North to marry a slave but he knew his words fell on deaf ears. George Sr. gave his son the money he had in his safe, $2,000.00, a covered carriage, and two horses. Jr. packed his trunk, gathered Aurora, and left his father's home and Louisiana. The couple made their way to Baltimore, Maryland, to a whites-only hospital. After 3 months of treatment, Aurora started to improve, and the light started to come back to her beautiful green eyes.

She started to look at Mr. Cotton as a kind man who had no stomach for slavery and realized the sacrifices, he made for her. He would come to her bedside every day with fruits for her body and flowers for her spirit. Within 6 months, she was able to leave the hospital. When Aurora was released from the hospital George picked her up in his carriage.

"I left Louisiana and I have forsaken my family. This was done because I love you and want to marry you. I told the doctor at the hospital you were going to be my wife once your sickness passed. Telling him that story, I was able to get you medical care that is reserved for whites," explained George Jr. They arrived at his room, and he got Aurora into bed.

"Thank you for saving my life. You have sacrificed so much for me, and I have treated you badly, I am sorry. I know you love me; you have proven that in so many ways," Aurora said in a sweet voice.

"Now that you understand everything, will you marry me?" Aurora sat up in the bed she said "yes". George sat at her bedside and kissed her hand.

George Cotton Jr. wanted to help newly freed slaves and make a home for his wife where she would always feel safe.

"There is a new town in Tennessee called Allen, where freed slaves have settled and built a town. This town will be a wonderful place to live and start a family," George said.

"I never want my children to feel less than human or be separated from me or sold," Aurora pleaded.

"I understand," he responded.

George and Aurora were married before they left Baltimore. They moved to Allen, Tennessee, where Mr. Cotton started the Town Center Bank. His financing helped the town to grow. Over the years the town prospered, and the Cottons welcomed a son, Victor Allen Cotton. He was privileged. He attended Howard University in Washington D.C., studying Law. He had returned to Allen in time for Jewel's party.

When the Cotton's arrived, the entire party stopped as everyone watched this striking couple and their handsome son enter the room. Mr. Cotton was dressed in a tailored suit of the time with gold stick pin and gold cufflinks, the light danced off his silver hair. His wife was as beautiful as ever. She wore a beautiful emerald-green dress with a gold sash and bustle; the green made her eyes look like jewels. Victor was the most handsome man Jewel had ever seen in her life, he was 6 feet tall, had beautiful skin the color of cream, he had his mother's green eyes and smile.

When Jewel greeted the family, Victor stepped in front of his mother and kissed her hand. Jewel was so taken aback she felt lightheaded. The Cottons had brought her a gift which she placed on the gift table and then guided them into the dining room. Once everyone started to read their place cards, Jewel noticed Victor move his card so that he would be sitting next to her; she felt lightheaded. Jewel ran to the Butler's Pantry to see if Father and Aunt Ida were ready for diner, they were. Aunt Ida smoothed her hair and straightened her dress. Father brushed off his jacket and they took their place at opposite ends of the dinner table; Jewel was at Father's right and Victor sat next to her. When the reverend asked everyone to bow their heads to bless the food, Victor took her hand in his and squeezed ever so lightly. Jewel thought, this man likes me, could he be the one?

Chapter 5

The Sunday after the birthday party seemed to be brighter for Jewel. She had dreamed about Victor all night and in her dreams, they were husband and wife. She dressed for Church and ran down the steps to meet her father so they could start on their way. Aunt Ida was at the breakfast table in her robe, she was upset with the way she was shunned at the party.

"I will never go to that church again. No one has any respect for me, they only tolerate me because of you and your position. No one respects me. I will never be accepted by these people, I'm finished trying," Aunt Ida said.

When Aunt Ida first came to town, she was a single woman without a family. She took up with several men in town and some of these men were married. Dr. Ira treated her when one of the men beat her up. He took her in as a housekeeper and after a few months, they were married. She told him she was pregnant, he believed her. When she didn't show signs of pregnancy, she confessed that she had lied. By then he had fallen in love with her, and he forgave her.

The town's people were a different story. They didn't know how she got him to marry her but there was all kinds of gossip. No one in town thought she was good enough for him. To ease the burden of the pregnancy lie she decided to bring Jewel into his life, to ease her conscious and soothe his feelings. Father believed in his marriage vows, "until death do us part." He is a God-fearing man. His prayers reflect this; Jewel was an answer to his prayer. He prayed for a beautiful baby girl. Jewel listened at the door of the dining room and was happy to hear Aunt Ida was not going to church with them. She was always in a hurry to leave the church and did not like to fellowship with members of the congregation. Father accepted what she said with quiet relief. Dr. Ira and Jewel started out the door for the buggy. It was such a beautiful day, they decided to walk. This was the first Sunday and that meant more people would be at church. The closer they got to the church, the more crowded the streets and sidewalks became. Everyone was dressed in their finest.

Jewel and Father stood out in the crowd because of his light blue suit with a yellow tie and yellow daisy in his lapel. Jewel's dress was pale pink. She wore a matching hat with small roses on the brim, she felt beautiful. When they started up the steps of the church, everyone greeted them with warm smiles and firm handshakes. Jewel could see the muscles in Father's face relax; he was on edge because of Aunt Ida's behavior at the party. No one missed Aunt Ida. Everyone was there to rejoice and praise the Lord, the past nights' events were now a faded memory. Once Jewel and Father had taken their seats in the pew, the organ started to play, the congregation stood and started to sing, it was a joyful noise. Reverend Cole led the choir in two more songs before starting his sermon. Jewel was listening very intently, Reverend Cole started to walk the aisles of the church as he preached. Jewel was watching and followed him with her eyes with great reverence as he preached and moved in his flowing robe. She turned to look down the middle aisle. Victor caught her eye, he smiled, and her heart started to pound. When church service ended, everyone went to the pasture behind the church to fellowship with punch and cake. Father was having a wonderful time speaking to the men and women. The small children were playing tag while the young adolescent boys and girls flirted with each other.

Jewel watched as Victor moved through the crowd of the town's most eligible young ladies. She didn't think he saw her watching him, but he did. He came over to Jewel with two glasses of punch.

"Will you join me in a cool drink?" Victor asked.

She took the cup into her trembling hands she tried to seem calm as possible. She was sure he could see how nervous she was.

"I enjoyed your birthday party. I had to leave early since my mother had a headache. There was so much I wanted to say to you," Victor said.

"What did you want to say?" Jewel asked as calmly as possible.

"I want to get to know you better. Do you think your father will let me call on you?" Victor asked boldly.

Jewel was so taken aback by the forward request she dropped her glass, it shattered, they both looked down and laughed. At that moment Father walked over to collect Jewel as it was time to head home.

"Sir, may I call on your daughter at your family's convenience?" Victor asked.

Father looked stern. Jewel's heart started to pound in her chest; she could hear it in her ears.

"Yes. That will be fine with me, Son," Father replied.

"May I escort Jewel to bible study on Wednesday?" Victor asked.

"Yes, and you are invited to dinner before going to bible study," said Father.

Victor gently kissed Jewel's hand. She could finally breathe. Father and Jewel said their goodbyes to the congregation and Reverend Cole and started their walk home; Jewel walked on air.

Chapter 6

Jewel was unable to contain her excitement about Wednesday. She would see Victor and he had permission to take her to bible study! This was the first time a young man had ever asked if he could call on her. She never thought herself good or pretty enough. Victor was from one of the most prominent families in Allen, she never thought he knew she was alive. She thought about her ancestors, who were royalty, then she calmed down because she was good enough for him no matter what the town thought. All day Wednesday Jewel fussed about what she would wear, her hair, and the menu. She asked Sadie to make one of her famous apple pies and cornbread for dinner. Jewel set the table with the best linens and crystals. The table was set for 4, she was unsure if Aunt Ida would come down for dinner, she had been in her room since the birthday party. Finally, it was 4 p.m. and everything was set for Victor's arrival. The doorbell rang, Father answered, Victor arrived with flowers for Jewel.

"Good afternoon, Sir," Victor said.

"Good afternoon, Victor. Jewel, come on down," Father said.

Father and Victor stood at the bottom of the steps. Jewel was a vision in blue, she had little sunflowers in her braided hair. When Victor saw her, he smiled and extended his hand.

"Good afternoon," he said.

Jewel stretched out her hand and he helped her down the last two steps.

"These roses are for you. Their beauty is pale in comparison to yours," Victor said as he presented her with a dozen red roses.

"Thank you," Jewel said.

She smiled at Victor, the 3 of them went to dinner. There was great conversation and food. Just as dessert was being served, Aunt Ida appeared at the dining room entrance. She was in her robe, her hair was a mess, she had been drinking. She started to swear at Father and Victor.

"No one is going to eat off my fine China," she screamed. Aunt Ida started throwing plates at the wall. Food and drinks went everywhere. Aunt Ida started to throw plates directly at Jewel. "You are a plague! You're my daughter and you treat me with contempt. But you love Ira and treat him like he's your real father," she continued to scream.

At that moment, tears welled up in Jewel's eyes as she looked at Father and Victor. The lie had finally been said out loud. Jewel felt her heartbreak for Father. Victor looked around the room at the two women and the broken man, he excused himself and slipped out the front door. Jewel ran upstairs, she felt her life as she had known it was over, she was sure Mother Ida would send her back to the farm, she was terrified. As she cried, it occurred to her how the lie would affect Father. She believed Mother Ida; she was sure father loved her. She wiped her eyes, left her room and sat at the top of the stairs. She listened to Father and Mother Ida. Father listened to Mother Ida as he looked around the room at the mess she had made with the dishes and food. What surprised Jewel was how calm Father was as Mother Ida talked.

"I have made so many sacrifices for you. I could have had any man in town, but I took pity on you! You have so much book sense that you have no room in your head for common sense," she screamed. "You have no idea how to keep a woman happy. Your performance in the bedroom is awful, you have never satisfied me!" she continued to scream. "I have been having an affair with Reverend Cole. What a joke on him and the town; the worst woman in town playing around with the holiest man in town."

"Jewel is my daughter. I left her with my mother when she was 6 weeks old. The only reason I brought her to Allen was to keep you from asking me to get pregnant again. Now, you have a child, and I can move into one of the spare bedrooms. Your touch makes my skin crawl!"

As she screamed and laughed, she danced around the room. Her breasts were exposed. Her robe fell to the floor, showing her completely naked body. Jewel thought, Mother Ida has gone crazy Father had to do something, he had to stand up for himself, but he just sat there with a blank stare on his face. Mother Ida continued to dance around the room, screaming how he was not a man. Father stood up; Jewel knew he was going to hit her. He walked over to his liquor cabinet and fixed himself a straight glass of bourbon whisky. He looked at Mother Ida, with pain and disbelief in his eyes.

"You think I don't know about you and Reverend Cole? That is the worst kept secret in town," he said.

Mother Ida stopped dancing. The shock of what he said sent a chill through Jewel's body. How could Father know this and never say a word? Mother Ida was also shocked; she sat down and started to cry.

"You knew?" She asked.

"Yes."

"How can you be a real man? Knowing another man is having your wife and do nothing," she said.

"I knew you were a whore when I married you," he said very calmly.

"You don't seem surprised that I'm Jewel's mother. How can you just stand there?" She screamed.

Father replied, "Ida my dear, I got a letter from your mother asking how Jewel was doing. Thanking me for taking in your daughter. She thought you had told me about Jewel. She said I must be a wonderful husband to take in a fatherless child and a woman with a questionable past. I am not the fool you think I am. I grew to love Jewel as my own flesh and blood. The fact that her mother is a whore is not her fault. Jewel has been a faithful, God-fearing daughter. How you produced such a child is a mystery to me."

Mother Ida stopped crying. She looked around the room, grabbing the last pieces of China, throwing them at the wall. She started her dance and screamed again. Father walked out of the room and started up the steps, he saw Jewel sitting on the steps with tears in her eyes.

"Don't cry, none of this is your fault. I love you more today than I did the day you came into my life. You will always be my daughter, no matter what may happen," Father said.

Jewel looked at him and buried her head in his chest, his strong arms and hands gave her support. Now that the lie had come to light, how would she live? What would Victor think of her knowing what her mother had done? Jewel felt she could have a future with Victor, or any decent man would never happen because of her mother. Father walked Jewel to her room and helped her to bed; he kissed her goodnight and closed her door.

Mother Ida continued to scream, dance, and break China. She then moved to the living room throwing and breaking anything, she could get her hands on. Sadie, who was working late to make the special dinner for Victor, had gathered her things and went out the back door when the screaming started. The neighbors heard it all; the confession of the affair and the confession that Jewel was her daughter and not her niece. By midnight, Mother Ida had destroyed the dining room and living room, Mother Ida was spent. She lay on the dining room carpet and listened to the neighbors' gossip about what they heard as they walked by.

Chapter 7

The morning was bright with sunshine, the birds were singing Jewel was looking out her bedroom window when there was a knock at the front door. This was unusual because all father's patients went to the clinic through the side door. Mother Ida was downstairs and opened the door. It was a telegram it held news about Grandmother Lizzie. As Mother Ida read the telegram she began to cry. Mary ran to Father to let him know about the telegram and how it made Ida cry. Jewel was standing behind the heavy parlor curtains she wanted to know what happened she realized it had to be something awful because she never saw Mother Ida cry. When he went into the parlor, she was sitting with a telegram in her hand.

He asked, "Is everything all right?"

She looked at him saying, "My mother died six weeks ago. The people from the church took her body and buried her in Potters Field. The church took over her property and sold it for $300 including her personal possessions, and the animals on the farm. They tore down the farmhouse. The church took the $300 to bury my mother and take over her land."

Father looked surprised, they never talked about her mother or the farm until it was decided Jewel was to come to live with them. Jewel listened and started to cry. Grandmother was mean and sometimes cruel, to die alone and have strangers take what little she had made her sad. She never went to church; these people were strangers. Jewel came from behind the curtains and sat at Mother Ida's feet, this was her grandmother a woman who cared for her, in her own way loved her as best she could. Mother Ida and Jewel cried. Father went back to his patients; he gave them space to grieve.

At dinner that evening Father asked Mother Ida, "Do you want to go to Indianapolis to see what really happened?"

"No, there is nothing to do. Everything is gone. It will only bring back bad memories. I have some peace of mind that she was buried, and I know what happened to her few possessions." Mother Ida said sadly.

"She is with God now. She is home," Jewel said as she looked up from her meal.

That was the last time anyone mentioned Grandma Lizzie. Over the next few weeks, Jewel stayed in her room as much as possible. She did not attend church; she was afraid of what everyone would say about her and Mother Ida. She wanted to see Victor. Father continued to see his patients, there was pity in everyone's eyes. Mother Ida took to her bed, taking meals in her room. During the night you could hear her cry, then go into a rage and start breaking things and turning over the furniture. There was nothing more in her room to break nothing was replaced only the bed and chest of drawers were left standing. Mary would try to clean the room Mother Ida would throw things.

"Do not go into her room, just leave her meals on the floor in front of her bedroom door," Father said.

It was now September; the dog days of August had ended. The days were becoming shorter, Jewel and Father enjoyed the cool evenings in the garden after dinner. They never talked about what happened that night in June, it now seemed like a distant memory. Mother Ida continued to stay in her room; she would eat and leave the empty tray outside her door. Mother Ida not coming out of her room started to seem normal. Father and Jewel went about their days, they had even returned to Church. Jewel never forgot Victor, she heard Mr. Cotton had sent Victor up North for the summer. Jewel didn't know why he was sent up North but was sure it had to do with the incident at the birthday party.

The 2nd Sunday in September was Reverend Cole's anniversary. He asked the congregation to forgive him for his affair with Ida, he even had a private conversation with Father who also forgave him. No one wanted to give any more thought to Mother Ida, the affair, or the bad behavior she displayed that night in June. The congregation embraced Father and Jewel. Mother Ida stayed away from the church to everyone's relief.

Reverend Cole's anniversary was a special day. The ladies of the church decorated the pews with fresh flowers everyone brought food for the afternoon diner in his honor. Sadie made several cakes and pies and farmers brought apple cider that had been put up for this special day.

The music at service was beautiful, Jewel sang, she felt happy and relaxed. Father also sang in his deep baritone voice; he was happier than Jewel had seen him in a long time. She looked around the church, it was full. The Cotton family was there, but no Victor. After service, everyone went outside to fellowship and eat. The tables were full of wonderful food, drink, and desserts from some of the best cooks in Allen.

Jewel spread out her blanket under a big oak tree next to the church and began to eat. This was her favorite spot on the church property. It was quiet and she liked the sound the leaves made when the wind blew. After her meal she leaned against the tree with her apple cider and closed her eyes, her thoughts immediately went to Victor. With her eyes closed, her mind drifted, she became aware she was not alone, she opened her eyes, standing in front of her was Victor, and he smiled. Jewel jumped and spilled cider on her dress, they both laughed.

"I missed church service because my train arrived late, but I'm happy I didn't miss the chance to see you," Victor said.

Jewel's heart started to beat hard, he took her hand and asked, "take a walk with me by the stream?"

Victor told her, "This summer, I have been able to clerk at a prestigious law office in Washington DC. DC is a magical city, the buildings, the people, the history, the freedom."

He continued to talk about his experience and all the things he had done but she wasn't listening. She could only think, she was on a walk with Victor Cotton, excited that she was alone with him. When they reached the stream, he took off his jacket and placed it on the grass for Jewel to sit, she felt like a queen. He continued to talk about his adventures over the summer. As he talked, Jewel looked deeply into his eyes. He stopped talking, looked at Jewel, leaned over, and gave her lips a sweet gentle kiss. Jewel froze. This was the first time she had been kissed; she had no idea how to respond.

"Is this your first kiss?" Victor asked. He sensed this.

"Yes," Jewel replied.

He smiled and began to talk about the different fish in the stream.

I'm acting like a child not responding more like a woman and freezing, Jewel thought to herself. Jewel heard Father calling for her; she jumped up, telling Victor, "I have to go!"

She ran toward Father's voice. Victor did not move, nor did he speak, he continued to sit next to the stream. On the way home, Jewel thought about the kiss. She was sure Victor had kissed more experienced girls. She decided the next time she was alone with Victor; she was going to prove to him she was a woman, and not a little girl.

Chapter 8

Winter came early to Allen with a blanket of snow that covered the town the week before Thanksgiving, it was beautiful. There was smoke from the fireplaces, children playing in the snow, and making snowmen. Everyone was happy anticipating Thanksgiving and most of all Christmas. Jewel watched the children from the living room window. She longed for the simple days when she was a child with no responsibilities and a light heart. Her heart was heavy with sadness for Father and the emptiness she felt because she had not seen or talked with Victor for weeks. Sadie was in the holiday spirit as she prepared the turkey dinner with all the trimmings, this year there would not be any guests, only Father, Ida, and Jewel. Father was still feeling the effects of Ida's hissy fit and did not want a repeat he thought it best not to invite anyone over for dinner.

"Can we invite the Cotton's over to the house during the holidays?" Jewel asked. She wanted to see Victor.

"The Cotton's will be out of town until after Christmas," Father said. Jewel was heartsick. Thanksgiving dinner was served, Mother Ida and Father sat at opposite ends of the table with Jewel in the middle, and there was very little conversation.

"There is a special church service this evening, Ida will you attend the service with me and Jewel?" Father asked.

Mother Ida sat and stared at Father; she didn't give him an answer but gave him a look that sent a chill up Jewel's spine. She made a slight smile that curled the ends of her lips. She got up, wiped her mouth, turned, and went up the stairs. Father shook his head, looked at Jewel, and gave her a reassuring smile. It started to snow as Father hitched the horse and buggy for church, Jewel caught snowflakes on her tongue. Father placed blankets in the buggy, they were warm. As they approached the church, they both began to relax from the tense Thanksgiving dinner. Jewel watched as the new snow twinkled like stars under the moonlight, she closed her eyes and pretended Victor was at her side, not Father. The church service was lively, with more music and singing for the Thanksgiving service. Jewel and Father sang and thanked God for all their blessing and good health.

After service everyone passed out the church door speaking and shaking hands, Reverend Cole was in his finest robe, he looked regal as he stood on the top step of the church. On the way home Father and

Jewel continued to sing, it was a perfect end to a day that started with so much tension. Over the weeks before Christmas Jewel went about taking care of the house and getting it ready for Christmas. She ordered bacon, sausages, cheeses, and fruits for Sadie to make into pies. She selected the best vegetables and stored them in the cool root cellar. There was ham and turkey on her list to purchase, once the food was purchased and stored, she turned her attention to decorating the house. There were evergreen branches placed on the fireplace mantel, with candles and bright red ribbons. She hung stockings for everyone in the house which included Sadie and Mary, she thought of them as family. Father was happy to see the extra stockings as he never considered Sadie and Mary as servants, Jewel decorated the dining room with evergreens, candles, and more ribbons.

    She placed candles in the front windows of the house and hung a large wreath with cranberries on the front door, everything was coming together beautifully. Jewel wanted to get the biggest Christmas tree she could find, so she started the week before Christmas looking for the perfect tree. She went to the Thompson farm; they were known for the beautiful spruce trees that grew on their property.

    When she arrived, she saw the Cotton's buggy parked next to the field of trees, her heart started to pound at the thought of seeing Victor. She parked her buggy, jumped out, adjusted her fur hat and coat, took a deep breath, put her shoulders back head up, she walked toward the field.

    Just as she walked through the gate, she heard Victor's voice, she turned, he gave her a quick kiss on the cheek, she was surprised and pulled away. Victors looked at her in amazement and asked, "Are you angry or upset with me?"

    Jewel thought about the question and in a very coy tone said, "Not at all, I have been too busy to be angry or upset with anyone."

    This was not the answer he expected, the ladies in Allen were always throwing themselves at his head, this was a new experience. Jewel walked through the field of trees inspecting them with great care; she knew how she wanted the tree to look. The tree was to be at least seven feet tall with all the branches even and full, no brown spots, and a large sturdy trunk. She went down the last row of trees, she found the one she wanted, Mr. Thompson cut it down. Jewel paid, the tree would be delivered at 6 p.m. Jewel walked toward her buggy and there stood Victor, he presented her with a small bough of mistletoe, he apologized for the unexpected kiss, she smiled and accepted his gift.

    He helped her into her buggy, as she settled into the seat, "Will I be able to call on you?" Victor asked.

"Yes." She snapped the reigns on the horses and drove away.

Jewel was excited when the tree was delivered. Even Mother Ida seemed moved by the tree. She directed Mr. Thompson to place the tree in front of the big bay window in the living room. Once it was in place, it was time to decorate. Mother Ida helped get the Christmas ornaments, ribbon, and bows down from the attic. She also helped Jewel put the tree in water and place the tree skirt around the bottom. They decorated the tree and sang Christmas carols; they also built a roaring fire. Father came in from the hospital and was surprised to see Ida out of her room helping Jewel decorate the tree.

Jewel helped father out of his coat, "Your dinner is in the oven. Once you get washed up, come to the table."

She set the table, placing his warm dinner in front of him. Father began to eat and look about the room at the decorations and the beautiful Christmas tree. He looked at Mother Ida, she had a soft look about her face in the glow of the fireplace. Father looked at her with a softness Jewel had not seen in months. He walked over and gave Mother Ida a kiss on her cheek. At that exact moment, she turned cold as ice. Her softness turned to a hard-evil expression. She turned and walked upstairs, once in her room she slammed the door so hard it was heard over the entire house. Father lowered his head, walked to the library, and closed the door. Jewel stood there with tears in her eyes, she thought, how could Mother Ida be so hateful during such a sweet moment.

Christmas Eve arrived with a gentle snowfall, as Jewel looked out her bedroom window there was a calm stillness to the early morning. She put on her robe, went down the steps to the kitchen, where the smell of freshly brewed coffee and Sadie's homemade biscuits filled the air. Jewel poured herself a cup of coffee. She sat in the kitchen nook drinking her coffee and daydreaming about Victor. Jewel finished her coffee and a biscuit with plum preserves, which Sadie had canned over the summer.

As she dressed, she continued to think about Victor. Father called out from the bottom of the stairs, "Ida, Jewel, come downstairs. I have a surprise for you!" Father exclaimed.

Gifts were all around the Christmas tree and Sadie had made the most wonderful eggnog, with a touch of Father's brandy. Jewel, Father, and Mother Ida drank eggnog in front of the fire. There was a knock at the front door, Father answered, it was Victor, and he had gifts for Father, Mother Ida, and Jewel. Father asked him in, he placed his gifts under the tree. Father offered him a cup of eggnog, asking him to take a seat. As the men settled in to talk Jewel and Mother Ida excused themselves and went into the kitchen to finish their drinks. Sadie had finished making pies, cakes, ham, and vegetables for Christmas dinner and was ready to leave. Jewel hugged her, wished her a Merry Christmas, and presented her with a Christmas gift from the family; Mary was also leaving and received her gift.

Mother Ida watched the two women interact with great jealousy, they never responded to her in such a fashion. This made her angry, she threw her glass of eggnog against the door as they left and walked up the back stairs to her room with not a single word said.

Jewel was stunned but Sadie and Mary were not surprised and were happy they didn't get hit on the way out the door.

"Jewel, is there a problem?" Father asked as he heard the glass break.

"No," she replied.

She cleaned up the broken glass and wiped eggnog off the wall. When she had the mess cleaned up, she sat in the dark kitchen and listened to the conversation between Father and Victor. She knew it was not polite to eavesdrop, but she wanted to know if Victor would talk to Father about her.

"Since I have graduated from Law School my parents are thinking about moving to Europe. They no longer want to live as second-class citizens in the United States."

"I understand, that may be a good move for them." Father said, "Being the only doctor in town, my conscience would not let me leave."

Jewel heard this and almost fell off the stool she was sitting on; she felt heartsick, she may never have the chance to tell Victor she loved him. That revelation scared her; she had never said that out loud. If she told Victor, how would he respond? Did he feel the same way? Her head started to spin, maybe it was the eggnog or the fact she admitted she loved Victor. Either way, she needed to talk to him. She quickly sliced the cakes and made a pot of coffee. When she had the tray, all set, she walked into the living room as if she never heard the conversation.

"Join me and Victor for coffee and cake Jewel. I am going to check on my wife. Be back shortly." Father smiled at Jewel as he started up the steps.

Once Father was out of the room, Victor moved close to Jewel, taking her hand. "I want us to be together. Do you feel the same way?" Victor asked.

"Yes" Jewel replied.

"I will ask Dr. Ira for your hand in marriage."

Jewel was elated and leaped into Victor's arms. They kissed a long soulful kiss. This was their first passionate kiss. Jewel felt this kiss proved she was not a little girl. After the kiss, he held her close, both were silent, she felt he loved her as much as she loved him. Before Father returned to the room, Victor went back to his chair across the room, Jewel smoothed her hair and was serving coffee when he walked into the room.

"I need to leave. We are having a family gathering," Victor explained.

He looked at Jewel, winked, and kissed her hand. Father then walked him to the door. When Jewel took the dishes back to the kitchen to tidy up, she walked on air. Victor wanted to be her husband. He wanted the dark, fatherless girl of a woman with a questionable reputation. She smiled.

Chapter 9

Jewel was excited for the New Year to begin. She would be married to the man she loved and have her own family, a family that no one could come between or harm. The New Year's Eve watch service would be mean more to Jewel this year because she was going to attend with her future husband and his family. As New Year's Eve morning arrived, Jewel fussed about her hair and what dress she would wear to service that evening.

"I will call for you at 3 p.m.," Victor explained, "we will join my parents in the family pew and after service, I will ask Dr. Ira for your hand in marriage. It will be a special night you will never forget."

As the clock ticked away, morning soon became late evening. As the sun set, an overwhelming feeling of fear started to churn in the bottom of Jewel's stomach. She had no confirmation of the plans she and Victor had made. Father had no communication with Victor or his family. Father was getting dressed to attend the watch service, she could hear him singing. The only thing she could do was imagine the worst, maybe Victor had been in an accident, or sick.

Father knocked at her door and asked, "Are you dressed for church? We need to leave in the next 10 minutes to be on time."

Jewel finished dressing, she hurried, as she thought, maybe I got the plan wrong, and we were to meet at church. Father and Jewel left the house and rode toward the church; she saw people she had never seen at church before. The watch service was very special to the people of Allen, TN. The watch service was held at all Negro churches because, during the time of slavery, the first day of the year was when Congress announced new laws that would take effect for the upcoming year.

This special church service was how all southern slaves heard the news of the Thirteenth Amendment to the Constitution had been passed to abolish slavery, January 31, 1865. This special service continues to be observed every New Year's Eve. We, as a people were free, by Federal Law, but in the hearts and minds of southern whites and even some whites up North, we were still slaves.

This fact was one reason Victor's family wanted to move to Europe where they could truly be free. The church was full of candlelight flickering, it was beautiful. As Jewel looked around the room, she didn't see Victor or his family, tears welled up in her eyes.

Father knew something was wrong with Jewel but when he asked, she said she was happy and ready to praise God for all her blessings. They settled into the pew, the choir entered, everyone stood and started to sing. After the choir had been seated, the late arrivals were ushered to their seats. Victor and his family were among the late arrivals. Jewel could finally breathe; she felt the weight of the world leave her shoulders. She started to sing with enthusiasm. Father saw her mood change; he was happy to see the tension leave her face. The watch service was full of song and praise, when it was over, everyone started to leave the church for the cold trip home.

Victor caught up with Jewel, he said, "I need to see you before morning, can I come to your house in an hour?"

Jewel could not imagine what he wanted but agreed to see him. Once home, Father came to her room, kissed her cheek good night, then went to his room. Jewel jumped out of bed put a candle in the window to let Victor know she was waiting for his arrival. Jewel waited but fell asleep; she was awakened by little stones being thrown at her window. She went to the window and there was Victor in the garden. When he saw her, he started to climb up the trellis. Once inside her room, Jewel led him to the fireplace to warm himself. Jewel looked at him with pure innocent love as he stood next to the fire.

"My family and I were late to service because we had an argument when I asked for their permission to marry. I told them I wanted to marry you," Victor explained, "my father said you were not suitable to marry."

"That girl is not good enough for you to marry. Her parents' background is questionable, as well as her bloodline," Mr. Cotton told Victor. "If you marry Jewel, I will cut off your allowance and you will have to leave my home."

Jewel could not believe what he was saying, heartbroken she continued to listen.

"I stood up to my father. I have left the family home and I am on my way to Washington, D.C. I have friends from college who will help me set up my law practice," Victor said, "I have come to say goodbye."

Jewel started to cry softly, her future with Victor was over before it began.

"This is the Cotton family Bible," he said as he showed it to Jewel. He placed her right hand on the Bible and placed a band of gold on her third finger left had. He said a prayer. In a quiet voice, Victor said, "In God's eyes, we are married."

"Are we really married?" Jewel asked.

Victor assured her, "Yes, we are. Once I move you to D.C., I will give you the grand wedding you deserve with all our family and friends."

Victor gave her a long deep passionate kiss; picked her up and laid her on the bed. He took off his clothes. Jewel thought he looked like a Greek statue she had seen in her schoolbooks as he stood in the candlelight. He came over to the bed and kissed her neck as he removed her nightshirt. She didn't want her new husband to think of her as a little girl, but a woman. She started to touch his body, in the same manner, he touched her. They lay facing each other; he kissed her neck and moved his hand down her body and between her thighs. He had found her special place, she had feelings she had never experienced. She laid back and moaned, he then moved her legs aside. While he changed positions, he was looking into her eyes as he started to enter her. First, there was pain then a sweet release. She started to moan and move around under Victor in a way that was unfamiliar, but natural. He moaned they both fell into each other's arms wet from the heat and sweat. As she lay in his arms, she felt like a real woman, she felt she had pleased her husband. Jewel fell asleep with a smile in her heart. Victor watched her sleep as he wrote her a farewell note, his smile changed into a sneer. He got dressed, grabbed the Bible, and went out the window.

A cold breeze swept over Jewel as she slept. She was not sure if what happened was real, or a dream. Jewel let down the window and looked at her bed, there was a blood stain on her sheets. She checked herself for her monthly and realized last night really did happen. This was the blood she heard would stain the sheets when a husband and wife were together on their wedding night. This was proof she was a virgin. Jewel smiled and wondered if Victor saw the blood before he left; he had proof she was his, and only his. The joy turned to panic when she thought about how she was going to get the sheets past Mother Ida and Mary. She hurried to get the sheets off the bed and down the back stairwell to the sink; she wanted to soak them before anyone came into the kitchen.

As she was finishing up the chore, Mother Ida came into the room asking, "What are you doing with sheets in the sink?"

Jewel replied, "My monthly started and soiled my sheets."

Mother Ida gave her a curious look, turned, and went back upstairs. She seemed to be satisfied with her explanation. With clean sheets, Jewel began to sing as she put them on her bed when she looked over and saw the note from Victor on her dresser.

Jewel,
Until I return from Washington, please keep our secret. I will be back for you.
Love,
Victor

Jewel could not understand why Victor wanted to keep their union a secret. She wanted to honor her husband and decided she would keep the secret.

Chapter 10

April started off warm and sunny, Jewel had not heard a word from Victor. When she saw his parents at church, they were polite but there was no mention of their son and Jewel was too afraid to ask. It was about the middle of April when she noticed every morning, she was sick to her stomach and was tired all the time. She also started to notice that she was gaining weight. Being the innocent she was, she had no idea she was pregnant. She thought it was the stress of missing Victor, that caused her missed monthly cycle and weight gain.

Father also noticed the changes in her body and asked her to come to his office. When she came into his office, she could see the worried look on his face when he asked her to sit down.

"How are you feeling? Is there anything you want to talk about?" Father asked.

Jewel started to cry and told her father everything that happened with Victor on New Year's Eve. His look of worry changed to compassion, and he pulled Jewel close to his chest as she cried. When the tears ended, Jewel started to understand what was happening to her. Without a word from Father, he led her to the examiner table to confirm his fears, she was indeed pregnant.

"I need to talk with Victor's parents, they should know what has happened, and they need to bring their son home to face his responsibilities," Father said with a tone she had never heard before.

Jewel pleaded "Please don't say anything to his parents. Victor said he will send for me when he is settled in Washington if you speak to his parents, he will know I did not keep our marriage a secret!"

"Married?" Father said, "What do you mean, married?"

Jewel was in tears as she told him about the Bible and prayers, she showed him the band on her left hand. "Victor said with the prayers and our hands on the Cotton Family Bible, we were married!"

Father looked at Jewel with pain and sadness in his eyes as he realized what Victor had done. He had lied to Jewel and stolen her innocence. "Victor lied to you, you are not married," Father said.

Jewel began to cry. As the tears locked under her chin, it was clear Victor never loved her. He only said what she wanted to hear, what a fool she was! They were not married and now she was pregnant. How could she face people? She was so ashamed.

"You will not be able to keep your secret hidden much longer because you are about three and a half months pregnant," Father informed her.

Jewel pleaded, "Please don't tell Mother Ida. I don't want to give her another reason to hate me."

"I will keep your secret," Father said as he left his office.

Jewel stayed behind and continued to cry on her knees alone.

The next day was Sunday and Father wanted the family to go to church, of course, Mother Ida said she had a headache and would not attend. This was wonderful news for Jewel as she was avoiding her mother as much as possible. She also felt a day out at church would do her some good and help her decide about her situation.

It was a beautiful sunny day, Jewel and Father decided to walk to church. There seemed to be more excitement than usual for a First Sunday. When Father and Jewel turned the corner towards the church, they saw a crowd around the Cotton's buggy. There was Mr. and Mrs. Cotton, and Victor. Jewel's heart started to pound so hard she felt sick, she stumbled. Father grabbed her arm.

"Gather yourself. Walk proudly and say hello to the Cotton's when we pass them," Father told Jewel.

As she passed Victor, he tipped his hat and smiled. Jewel thought she would faint, but Father held her tightly by the arm as they went into the church to their usual seats. The organist started to play, and the late arrivals rushed to their seats. The Cotton Family proceeded to their reserved pew at the front of the church. Jewel prayed, keeping her eyes closed through most of the service.

She could not bear to look at Victor when she thought of her situation, the lies, her eyes filled with tears.

Towards the end of service, there were announcements, Reverend Cole asked Mr. Cotton to come to the front of the church. A hush went over the entire church. Mr. Cotton walked proudly to the front of the church then turned to address the congregation and motioned for his son to join him.

Jewel thought Victor looked so handsome, tall, and more mature than she had remembered. He had grown a mustache. Mr. Cotton shook his hand when he arrived at the front of the church.

"My son Victor has graduated from Howard University with a Law Degree, he is to join a historic law firm in Baltimore, Maryland," Mr. Cotton said proudly.

The congregation stood up with loud applause and praises to the Lord. Mr. Cotton then asked for everyone to be seated, there was more. Victor then looked to the family pew and next to his mother was a beautiful girl, very fair-skinned, wearing a sky-blue suit with a matching hat. Her long blonde curls bounced as she walked toward Victor. He met her, extended his hand to help her up the step. Once there he embraced her. Mr. Cotton looked on as Victor released his embrace but kept his arm around her waist and announced

"Miss. Ruth York of Baltimore, Maryland, is engaged to marry my son Victor Allen Cotton June 15th at her family's home in Baltimore, Maryland."

The crowd erupted with praise, dancing in the aisle, the organist played, everyone rushed to the pulpit to offer congratulations and to shake hands with the father and son. Jewel just sat, staring, unable to move or utter a word. Father saw the look in her eyes and quickly got her to her feet, they left the church as if they were thieves in the night.

Once home Jewel was still in shock, unable to speak. Father undressed her and lay her in her bed, tears ran down her face, she found it difficult to breathe. When she could cry no more, Jewel continued to lay in bed staring at the ceiling, she refused to eat. Father tried to give her broth, she turned it away. She wanted to be alone. She thought she wanted to die.

Days passed; Jewel would not leave her room. Father became increasingly worried for Jewel and the new life she carried. He decided to tell Mother Ida, hoping she would talk to their daughter. He told her the entire story, to his surprise, Mother Ida cried. Mother Ida made tea and Jewel's favorite sandwiches, put them on a tray, went to Jewel's door, and knocked softly.

"May I come in?" Mother Ida asked.

Jewel was surprised because she would normally just open the door and come in. Jewel answered, "Yes."

Jewel was on her back staring at the ceiling, the heavy drapes were closed blocking the morning sun. Mother Ida opened the drapes and placed the tray on Jewel's bedside table. Mother Ida then went across the hall, brought a basin of water, clean towels, and soap back to Jewel's room, and proceeded to wash her face and hands. As she did this, both women cried. Jewel was shocked at Mother Ida's tears; she was being so kind and treating her like a daughter. The women did not speak. Mother Ida poured the tea and watched Jewel eat and drink, she was pleased. After the tea had been drunk and the sandwiches were eaten, Mother Ida set the dishes aside, she pulled up a chair next to Jewel's bedside and began to tell her a story.

"There was a very young and innocent girl who fell in love with the wrong man, who told her he loved her, and that they would be married. She found herself pregnant and alone, the man left her in a rooming house with no money, miles from her family. The owner of the rooming house gave her a job working in the kitchen for food and a room. The only money she made was selling herself to the men who came to rent rooms by the hour or day. When she had enough money saved for a bus ticket, she took herself and her baby girl home to her family's farm. The family was so ashamed of her they told her to leave but the baby could stay. She did as was ordered. She lived from hand-to-mouth and man-to-man for years until she met a kind doctor who loved her and married her."

It was at that moment Jewel realized Mother Ida was talking about herself and she was the baby left on the farm. Mother Ida was not evil or mean, she was hurt and broken. For the first time, Jewel understood her mother and grandmother's motivations. She continued to cry with Mother Ida. When Mother Ida left the room, Jewel got up, looking out the window her path seemed clear, she would leave Allen before she brought further shame to her mother and father. Jewel felt after her talk with Mother Ida, she was able to pray again. She found the strength to leave her room and venture downstairs for meals with Father and Mother Ida.

"Don't leave Allen. Stay here with your family. Your mother and I will help you raise your baby," Father said.

"The town will shun Jewel and the baby. I don't want Jewel to leave, but for her to keep some pride it will be best for her to leave," Mother Ida said.

Father and Jewel saw the wisdom in what she was saying and despite the fear of the unknown, Jewel knew she would have to make a life for her and her child away from Allen and the Cottons. It was the end of May and Jewel felt her baby move for the first time, all her clothes were getting tight and with summer on the way, she would no longer be able to wear sweaters and jackets to hide her growing belly. Father's sister lived in Murfreesboro, Tennessee, where she owned a dry goods store. She agreed to take Jewel in and help her through the last months of her pregnancy.

One of Father's grateful patients, Mr. Casey, would take her to Murfreesboro. Mr. Casey had broken his leg while working on his farm. He was not married and was found days later in the field by a neighbor. When he arrived in Allen for treatment, he was taken to Dr. Ira. It was then decided he would stay with Dr. Ira for round-the-clock treatment. Because of Dr. Ira's kindness and skill, Mr. Casey did not lose his leg. This incident started a long, dedicated friendship with Mr. Casey.

Aunt Ivy's store served the Negro families in Murfreesboro. Her husband and two sons were killed in a fire at their home, she now lived above the store. Aunt Ivy was all alone, she welcomed Jewel and the promise of a new life.

Jewel said goodbye to all that were close to her in the house. Sadie made her food for the trip and Mary made her some large tops to accommodate her belly. Mother Ida hugged her goodbye as did Father. They all cried as the buggy got smaller and smaller in the distance. It was an 8-hour buggy ride to Murfreesboro. Jewel felt hopeful as the buggy rolled and bounced over the road to her new home. She had no idea what to expect but she knew she was keeping her baby with her at all costs and becoming a mother the baby could love with pride.

Chapter 11

The sun was hot and unforgiving this day in July 1932, for the buggy ride to Murfreesboro, Tennessee. The ride was very uncomfortable for a 6-month pregnant Jewel. Mr. Casey was very kind and stopped as often as she needed. The drive seemed to take forever, but when she saw the Cumberland River, she knew she would not have much further to go. Jewel and Mr. Casey arrived in Murfreesboro around 6 a.m. on a quiet Sunday morning.

    Aunt Ivy was expecting them and had a hot breakfast waiting. The dry goods store was cheerful with two big windows that faced the street with yellow curtains at the windows. Inside were barrels of flour, sugar, salt pork, and the shelves were filled with glass jars of tobacco, candy, and some items Jewel had never seen before. There were tools for the farmers, bolts of cloth for the women to make clothes, and Bibles. As Jewel was helped down from the buggy by Mr. Casey, Aunt Ivy came out the door to greet them. Jewel could smell the bacon and coffee from upstairs.

    Aunt Ivy was a spry woman 65 years old. She was the beautiful color of golden Autumn leaves you would see on a Maple tree. Her hair was pulled back in a tight bun of black and silver, her eyes were blue, and there was wisdom etched in her face. She was a small woman with a bounce in her walk that made her look younger than her years. She was wearing overalls and a blue shirt with rolled sleeves, a white apron, but she was not wearing shoes. Jewel would later learn that Aunt Ivy never had shoes growing up and found them to be a nuisance, she would rather be barefoot. She enjoyed the feel of the ground under her feet, and only wore shoes to church.

    Once inside, Jewel and Mr. Casey were guided to the back stairs that led to the living quarters upstairs. They were guided to the kitchen for breakfast bacon, eggs, potatoes, biscuits, and hot coffee with sugar and cream. Jewel looked around her new surroundings and saw a small sitting room off the kitchen. She ate her fill and talked to Aunt Ivy about her brother, Mother Ida, and her trip. She never asked Jewel any questions about her situation, she was too kind to ask in front of Mr. Casey. After the last biscuit was eaten, Mr. Casey went down to the street and removed Jewel's trunk from the buggy, hauled it upstairs, and placed it in the bedroom she would share with Aunt Ivy. Jewel and Aunt Ivy packed him sandwiches and jars of water for his trip back to Allen.

Aunt Ivy gave him a letter for Father. As the morning sun raced across the sky, Jewel watched him ride away into the distance. She didn't know if she should be relieved or cry for what she was losing, she knew she had to be strong for herself and her baby. For the first time, Jewel looked around the bedroom. She was to share this room with Aunt Ivy and eventually her new baby. It was a cozy space that had a fireplace on one wall with a mantel filled with pictures from Aunt Ivy's marriage and her sons. The pictures stood as a testament to love lost. This made Jewel very sad, she started to cry as she looked at the wedding picture of Aunt Ivy and her husband how happy and young, they looked. Jewel felt this was something she would never have, a husband and a home of her own. Having a baby without a husband was the worst shame a woman could bring on herself and no decent Christian man would ever want her. As she cried, Aunt Ivy came into the room and hugged her.

"Everything will work out, stay prayerful. The Lord will send you a husband. He will be a wonderful father to your baby." Ivy said "Plans needed to be made. I need help with the dry goods store. Sunday the store was closed, everyone goes to Church."

Aunt Ivy missed Sunday service to get Jewel settled and give her time to rest. Monday thru Saturday the store was open from 8 a.m. to 6 p.m. her little store also served as a meeting place for the older men in the community who no longer worked the fields.

They came, sitting out front, playing checkers, talking about their youth, gossiping like little old ladies. This struck Jewel as funny, men gossiping. Jewel was dead-tired after her journey from Allen, so she did not hear the rooster crow or stir when Aunt Ivy got up. It was the wonderful smell of baking bread that had finally awakened her. Jewel jumped up, poured water in a basin, washed quickly, dressed, and met Aunt Ivy in the kitchen.

"Good morning," Ivy said with a smile as she poured a glass of milk for Jewel along with a slice of fresh bread and butter.

Aunt Ivy baked bread, she also made cakes and pies to sell in her store, her cakes and pies were so good, that some of the white families would send their maids to buy them for special occasions or as a treat for their family. It was almost 8 a.m. and Aunt Ivy went downstairs to open the store, she asked Jewel to tidy up before she came down for her first day as a clerk in a dry goods store. Jewel had never had a "job" this was an adjustment, standing on her feet for 10 hours, helping customers, packing bags, stocking, and not to mention meeting the townspeople in her condition. The first day was the worst but as the days and weeks passed, Jewel was able to work and not get as tired as she had in the beginning.

She went to church every Sunday with Aunt Ivy. Jewel decided to join the church, she confessed to the congregation her circumstances. How she became pregnant, with no husband, and living with Aunt Ivy in Murfreesboro. To her surprise, none of the congregation shunned her, there was no judgment, she was embraced by the church and was told, "you have a home, we are your new family." This touched Jewel, she also thought about going back to Allen. When she mentioned this to Aunt Ivy, she showed Jewel a letter she had gotten from her brother. The letter said:

> *Victor and his new wife have moved back to Allen for the birth of their first child. I will deliver the baby she is having problems and the Cotton's felt the weather and surroundings in Allen were more accommodating.*

Jewel realized she could never return to Allen. Victor was truly out of her life. As sad as she was, she did not cry, she did not feel sorry for herself, she was looking toward her future. Allen, Tennessee, and Victor were her past.

Chapter 12

Jewel saw the local Negro physician, Dr. Pratt, he said the baby was due at the end of October. Aunt Ivy asked one of the local carpenters to make a crib for the baby as a surprise. It was made of dark cherry wood and rocked back and forth; Jewel thought this was the most beautiful thing she had ever seen. Jewel made some baby clothes, blankets, and diapers. She had been given some baby clothes from the ladies at the church. Jewel was in good health, she was happy, she was ready for her baby's arrival. It was now the first of October and Jewel had started to have swollen ankles and backaches. Aunt Ivy stopped her from working in the store, so she stayed upstairs knitting and watched the people come and go from the upstairs window.

The postman came with a letter from Mother Ida, the first since she left Allen. In the letter she wrote:

> *Victor's wife was horseback riding she was thrown and lost the baby. Mr. and Mrs. Cotton feel she fell on purpose. After the fall it was discovered, she will never be able to have children. She moved back to Baltimore once she was able to travel, Victor is in Allen all alone. Jewel this may be your only chance to come home. You need to let the Cottons know you have their grandchild; this may be the only one they may ever have.*

Jewel agonized over the letter for days. She also discussed Mother Ida's thoughts with Aunt Ivy who read the letter.

"I think you will be better off not telling the Cotton family you have their grandchild. With their money and position, they may try and take the baby. When it comes to Victor, do you want a man who was trapped by the obligation of a baby? A man who does not love you?" asked Aunt Ivy.

Jewel still loved Victor and she wanted him to know he was a father. She felt once he saw the baby, he would realize he loved her, want to marry her, and make a family. Aunt Ivy did not agree with what Jewell was thinking, she wanted her to stay in Murfreesboro, Tennessee.

Later that night Jewel felt sick, she got up to go to the bathroom and her water broke, she screamed. Aunt Ivy heard the scream. She jumped out of bed and helped Jewel back to her bed where she went into labor. Jewel continued to labor and when the sun came up, Aunt Ivy was able to contact Dr. Pratt. Jewel had been in labor for 15 hours, with no baby. The baby is breached, which was causing problems with the delivery. Dr. Pratt sent word to the local midwife to come quickly and help with the delivery. Once the midwife arrived, she and Dr. Pratt were able to turn the baby and Jewel delivered a healthy baby girl. She named her Victoria May Johnson; Jewel was 17 years old and a mother. The baby weighed 6 pounds, 10 ounces. She had a full head of beautiful dark hair. Her complexion was a combination of Victor's cream color and Jewel's dark hue and had Jewel's gray eyes. She was born on October 21, 1932, at 9 a.m.

Aunt Ivy gave Victoria her first bath. She was wrapped in a fluffy pink blanket with a matching hat. The midwife helped Jewel out of bed to wash and have her bedding changed. Once Jewel was back in bed, Victoria took to her breast with great vigor. Jewel watched her daughter nurse when she realized, this tiny person will be loved unconditionally with or without Victor. She smiled and held the little bundle closer. Baby Victoria was thriving! She was gaining weight and she smiled when she heard her name, she was a beautiful little girl.

When Victoria was 6 weeks old, Mother Ida arrived driven by Mr. Casey. She had baby gifts from Father and members of the church in Allen. When Mother Ida saw the baby, she knew what Jewel had told her was true, Victor Cotton was the baby's father. She had his chin and nose. Aunt Ivy welcomed her with a big hug, invited her upstairs where they all enjoyed dinner and one of Aunt Ivy's pies. After dinner, Mother Ida held the baby and started to cry, she was looking at her first grandchild.

"I want this baby to have a better life than you or I had," Mother Ida said with tears in her eyes. "You need to return to Allen. She is a Cotton. She should have her birthrights no matter what happens between you and Victor. You need to return to Allen and present the baby to the Cotton family. Once they see her, they will know she is Victor's daughter."

"I want what is best for Jewel and Victoria," Aunt Ivy protested. I don't see the Cottons claiming Victoria, but if going back to Allen to see Victor and his family make you happy, I am behind you. "

It was coming up on Thanksgiving, Mother Ida was anxious to get home. Mother Ida and Aunt Ivy packed, bundled the baby and Jewel in blankets, coats, and gloves for the cold ride back to Allen. Mr. Casey loaded Victoria's crib on the back along with Jewel's trunk and they were on their way. There were no conversations during the ride, it was a cold silent buggy ride back to Allen.

This gave Jewel time to dream about telling Victor he had a beautiful daughter. In her dream, he would ask for her forgiveness, ask her to marry him, and his family and the town would embrace her and Victoria with love and acceptance.

The first snow of the season had just started to fall when they arrived in Allen. The town looked magical as the morning sun started to rise. When the buggy stopped in front of the house, Father greeted Jewel with a long warm hug, he welcomed her home. Jewel and Mother Ida were ushered into the kitchen, where Sadie and Mary greeted them with warm smiles.

Mr. Casey unloaded the buggy and with help from Father, the crib was taken upstairs to Jewel's old room and placed next to her bed. Downstairs the women unwrapped Victoria from her blankets as she lay on the kitchen table. When the last blanket was removed from the baby's head, she smiled and reached up for her mother. All the women started to cry at the sight of such a sweet innocent face. Father came in, this was his first time seeing the baby. Tears welled up in his eyes, everyone was moved by the sight of this little baby girl. Jewel went upstairs to her old room which she was to share with her baby girl. As she sat in a rocking chair by the window overlooking the garden, she began to remember the night Victor came to her. Her eyes filled with tears, and they rolled down her cheeks and dropped gently on Victoria as she nursed. This little girl was a Cotton, she was Victor's firstborn. She thought about how she was going to present the baby to him or let Mother Ida and Father speak with Victor's parents. She rocked Victoria and felt her tug at her breast, she had finished nursing.

There was a soft knock on her door, Mother Ida opened the door to tell her dinner was ready. She buttoned up her dress, washed Victoria's face, and composed herself for the family dinner. After dinner, Jewel took the baby to the parlor where there was a rocking cradle for Victoria. Father had one of the local carpenters make it special for the baby, her name was carved on the headboard. Father poured a glass of hard cider for Jewel and Mother Ida; she knew they were going to talk about the baby.

"Jewel, do you want to tell the Cotton family about Victoria? Are you prepared to face Victor and his parents?" Father asked. Mother Ida looked anxious.

"I want to introduce Victoria to her father; he can make the decision to tell his family," Jewel replied.

"I don't agree with only telling Victor. You should tell his parents first and have them talk to Victor." Mother Ida interjected.

Jewel stood her ground, "I want to see Victor alone and present Victoria."

Father said, "I understood your need to see Victor alone. You want him to accept and love Victoria without being pushed by his parents to accept her and the baby."

Mother Ida finally gave in and would respect Jewel's wishes. Father was to see Mrs. Cotton the next morning, she had taken to her bed after Victor's wife had her miscarriage and left her son. She was heartsick more than anything, she knew how much her son was hurt by the actions of his wife. Victor had not gone back to Baltimore to pursue his Law Career, he remained in Allen to be close to his family.

"I will invite Victor back to the house for coffee under the guise of giving him advice to help his mother. This will give you a chance to tell Victor about his daughter," Father said.

Chapter 13

Jewel watched the sun rise as Victoria slept, knowing today would be the day she would see Victor and he would learn he was a daughter. Jewel was anxious as she heard the baby cry for her breakfast. She sat in the rocking chair dreaming Victor would take Victoria in his arms and love her then thank her for such a beautiful healthy baby. She dreamed Victor would ask for forgiveness, tell his parents he loved her and the baby, and wanted to marry Jewel she would be accepted by his family, and they would start their lives together. Mother Ida interrupted her dream when she knocked to ask her to come down for breakfast. Father was sitting at the table eating toast and drinking coffee as Jewel sat down with the baby.

"Jewel," he said, "are you sure you want to see Victor alone to tell him about Victoria?"

"Yes," she replied as she hugged Victoria.

Father finished his coffee, kissed Mother Ida, patted the baby's head, got his medical bag, and left the house. Jewel expected Victor at 11 a.m. she wanted to look her best and she wanted Victoria to shine. She dressed in her best dress and braided her long black hair the same way she wore it the first day they met. Victoria was cute in a little pink dress that Aunt Ivy had made for her. She went down to the parlor, placed the baby in the crib, and sat next to her, she was ready to see Victor.

"Do you want me to sit with you while you wait for Victor?" Mother Ida asked.

Jewel replied, "No."

Mother Ida kissed the baby's cheek and went upstairs. The clock started to chime, it was 11 a.m. Jewel heard Father and Victor talking as they came in the front door. Jewel stood up, went to the door, and greeted Father and Victor. Father looked at Victor, who looked stunned to see Jewel, he stopped talking and looked at her as if she was a stranger. Jewel took their coats and ushered them to the parlor for coffee and sandwiches. Victor remained silent as he took a seat. Jewel gave him a cup of coffee."

"Would you like a sandwich?" she asked Victor. He continued to stare in stunned silence.

"Please give me a sandwich, I am starving. It has been a busy morning," Father said.

Father, with his sandwich and coffee, sat on the sofa and tried to engage Victor in conversation. Jewel sat next to Father. Victoria was next to them in her crib. Jewel tried to read the expression on Victor's face as the silence lasted for what seemed like hours. When Victoria started to cry, Father looked at Jewel and excused himself, he patted Jewel's hand for assurance and walked to the kitchen. Jewel was alone with Victor and their daughter. The baby continued to cry; Victor did not speak he continued to stare. Jewel picked up Victoria, she walked and bounced the baby to quiet her. Victor continued to stare. Finally, he stood up approached Jewel, took the baby in his arms, and placed her in the crib.

Turning to face Jewel, with a face of pure hate and anger he said, "Your Father asked me here today to discuss my mother and you appear out of nowhere."

Jewel could not believe the way he was attacking her, "What do you mean? This is my home," she replied.

"This baby, where did she come from?" he screamed.

"She is your daughter. She was conceived the night you told me we were married," Jewel said.

Victor walked over to the crib and looked at Victoria, he turned and said, "Do you expect me to believe that baby is mine? If you want to soothe your guilt and shame by telling yourself the one night, we laid together we were married, you must be a bigger fool than I thought. I said what you wanted to hear so I could have sex with you. I never cared for you, what a joke. Do you think I would ever bring someone like you home to meet my family? or taint my bloodline? You are the daughter of the town's whore. Do you even know who your father is?" Victor screamed.

Jewel started to cry but her hurt quickly turned to anger and she lashed out saying, "I am not the whore. It appears your wife was the whore. She sold herself cheap, to become your wife, killed your baby, and left town. You, Sir, are the fool!

This baby was conceived in love, on my part, and she will never know her father did not want her. I can't believe I thought you loved me, or that I loved you. You don't deserve me or Victoria. I've sinned, but the Lord knows that I was innocent along with Victoria. You will reap what you have sowed. You will die alone and never know the love of a child, or a good woman." Jewel fought back her tears.

Father heard the loud voices and Victoria crying; he came back to the parlor. He asked Victor to leave. Victor grabbed his coat and slammed the door. At that moment Victoria stopped crying and Jewel realized she was alone and solely responsible for the love and care of her baby, and herself.

She looked at Father, Mother Ida had come downstairs as Victor slammed the door. Mother Ida held her daughter as she cried with long, deep sobs as if someone had died. In Jewel's mind, Victor had died. Jewel lay on her bed, staring at the ceiling as the events of the day played in her mind over and over. Victor was right, she was a fool, but she was not weak. She was much stronger than anyone knew. She would make a home for herself and Victoria. She knew she would need to leave Allen and her family. She thought of where she could go and begin her new life. She wanted to go to a place where no one knew her. A city, not a small town; she decided to go to Nashville, about twenty-five miles from Murfreesboro.

The holidays brought a quiet joy to the family. It was Victoria's first Thanksgiving and Christmas. Jewel and Mother Ida helped Sadie prepare the Thanksgiving feast which included a large turkey, ham, and all the fixings. Sadie made her famous cakes and pies. There were no guests this year only Father, Mother Ida, Jewel, and Victoria. The small family sat down to eat with Victoria in her crib. There was some anticipation of the prayer Father would give but he prayed as usual and asked for Victoria to be blessed. Dinner was eaten and enjoyed but there was little conversation. Jewel felt she had brought sadness to her family, and she regretted doing so.

Christmas was Jewel's favorite time of year. When it was time to decorate for Christmas, there was sadness, she would not attend church or leave the house to shop. Her spirit was crushed, and nothing seemed to cheer her up, not even the giggles and coos from Victoria.

Jewel made the decision to leave Allen right after Christmas. The memory of Victor bedding her on New Year's Eve was too much to bear. She planned to leave on December 28, 1932. Plans were made for her departure; baby clothes were gathered for Victoria and Jewel's trunk was packed for the long journey to Nashville.

Mr. Casey agreed to take them, just as he had taken them to Murfreesboro. He had purchased a used pick-up truck so the small family would not be cold or exposed to the elements as they had been when traveling by horse and buggy.

This time there would be no Aunt Ivy. There was no one to greet her; she was completely on her own. Father gave Jewel $300 and a letter of introduction as a maid. She would have when she looked for a job.

The day to leave finally arrived. Father, Mother Ida, Sadie, and Mary all gathered on the front stoop to say goodbye, it was cold and windy. The weather magnified the sadness. Jewel did not cry as the truck left Allen, she held Victoria close to her breast, prayed, and held her head high as they passed the last house leading into Allen, she would not look back.

Chapter 14

January 2, 1933, was a cold snowy day when Mr. Casey pulled into Nashville with Jewel and Victoria. He took them to a boarding house in East Nashville where Jewel was greeted by the owner. Jewel met Mrs. Cook, but everyone called her Big Momma. She was a dark, heavy-set woman who had three sons. Her husband worked as a cook at the largest white hotel in downtown Nashville. He came home on Tuesdays, his one day off, to see his family. Her sons were married and lived on a farm in Pulaski, Tennessee, as sharecroppers. The family would come to Nashville for Christmas with their wives and her grandchildren.

Mr. Casey helped Jewel with her trunk, Big Momma showed her to the room she was renting. The room was warm and cozy with a queen-size bed, side table, lamp, dresser, and a wardrobe for her extra clothes. The window in her room looked over the backyard. She pictured herself having a picnic with Victoria when the weather was warm, and all the flowers were in bloom.

Once Mr. Casey placed her things in the room, Jewel gave him a hug and thanked him. He was down the steps on his way back to Allen in one swift move. Jewel paid Big Momma $12 for a month's stay in advance and went to her room. She was alone in her room with the baby. She looked around, looked at Victoria, and started to cry. She felt homesick already. She was sad and angry at the same time. Her anger was directed at Victor for the way he had treated her and their daughter. She knew in her mind she should forgive him, but her heart was broken; she did not think she would ever be able to forgive him. Jewel got the baby changed, fed her, and laid down next to her in the big comfortable bed. She had a comforter Mother Ida had given her, which smelled of her perfume. The smell brought back sweet memories of Allen as she fell asleep.

The morning sun greeted Jewel and Victoria along with the smell of biscuits and coffee; she didn't realize how hungry she was. She dressed herself and the baby, went down the back steps to the kitchen where Big Momma had made breakfast for all her borders who were gathering at the table. There was Mr. Bill, an older man who moved in after his wife died; two students, John and Michael, who were attending Meharry Medical College. Gladys, who worked as a maid and May, who worked as a cook.

The East Nashville area had big homes owned by some of the wealthier white families in the city, this was good news for Jewel. Many of the homes were in walking distance of the boarding house. After breakfast Jewel returned to her room and started to think about getting a job to support herself and Victoria, she would ask Big Momma for her advice. When Victoria fell asleep, Jewel placed her between four pillows covered her lightly with the comforter and went downstairs to see Big Momma. Jewel walked into kitchen as she was gathering food for the evening meal, she did not cook lunch because everyone was either at school or work. She was singing Wade in the Water, Jewel joined in, they both sang at the top of their lungs and started to laugh at the end. Jewel felt more at home than she had ever before. She asked Big Momma about Nashville.

"East Nashville is a quiet place with no problems for the Negros who lived here. We stay on our side of town that is divided by Main Street. The white people live on the other side, they own the big houses that overlook the Cumberland River." Big Momma explained to her.

Jewel asked, "Do you know anyone that can watch Victoria while I look for work?"

Big Momma laughed. "Honey child, I was waiting for you to ask me to watch that pretty baby girl. I had boys and always wanted a girl!"

This made Jewel happy to know she would have a good person watching over her baby while she worked.

Big Momma said, "The Clark family was looking for a girl, they live about two miles away."

Jewel got the address and decided she would go to their home early the next day. It was a good day to walk to the Clark home, the sun was shining, and the snow had melted. Jewel dressed warmly as possible, she got Victoria dressed and took her to Big Momma, who was excited to see Victoria, she smiled and cooed. Jewel was out the door walking up the hill to the Clark's home, the warm sun felt good on her face. When she arrived at the house, she thought how it reminded her of Mother Ida and Father's home in Allen, it had a big wrap-around porch. She rang the doorbell which was answered by Tim who was the butler, he wore a black suit and white gloves, Tim was surprised to see this colored girl at the front door. Before she could say a word, Tim stepped out on the porch grabbed her arm, he took her to the side yard.

"Little girl, why is you knocking on the front door? Don't you know all colored people go to the back door? Only white people can come through the front door," he said.

Jewel was stunned, this was her first time being treated in such a manner. All the homes in Allen were owned by colored families and she had always gone in the front door.

"I didn't know to go to the backdoor, I'm sorry, I'm here for work." Jewel explained.

Tim squinted his eyes saying, "You is now in a different place. Colored people got to watch what they say and do to keep the peace. You need to take low and stay out of the white man's way to survive."

Jewel nodded and was taken to the back door by Tim, she was met by May from the boarding house.

"Keep an eye on her. Tell her what she needs to do to get work. Keep quiet, smile, and always say yes ma'am and no ma'am," Tim said.

May nodded and took Jewel into the kitchen by a large fire where she was able to sit and warm herself. Jewel knew she had a lot to learn about this new city she was going to call home, she had to make good for Victoria's sake. After she was warm May asked, "Are you here for the maid's job?"

"Yes," Jewel replied.

"If that's what you want," May explained, "then you need to understand the rules of the house. First, Mrs. Clark likes to give big parties with lots of music and food. Mr. Clark is a lawyer and works very late. The two children, twin girls Becky and Lucy, are away at college. They come home for holidays and breaks. Mrs. Clark is the main one you will need to please, she is a kind woman but fussy, just do what she tells you."

Jewel nodded her head and asked, "Will I be able to see Mrs. Clark today?"

"Yes," May replied. She left the kitchen to get Mrs. Clark and tell her why Jewel was there.

Jewel took off her hat and smoothed down her hair and brushed her clothes. Mrs. Clarke came into the kitchen, and Jewel stood up to greet her. Jewel gave her the letter from Father, which she read, she asked Jewel

"Are you able to start right away? Your pay will be $5 per week. You can eat whatever is left over from our meals and you must keep your uniform clean, I will give it to you. Do you understand?"

"Yes ma'am," Jewel said.

Mrs. Clark asked Jewel to follow her. Mrs. Clark was a pretty woman with blonde hair and blue eyes. Her blue eyes reminded Jewel of the summer skies over Allen. She showed Jewel to a closet that had several uniforms for the maids. She tried on several before she found her size. She was looked over by Mrs. Clark who proceeded to tell her of her duties.

"Your day will start at 7 a.m. and end at 6 p.m. Your off day is Sunday. You will make the beds, change linen as needed, dump chamber pots, and help me get ready for my parties. You will do general housekeeping, as well as wash and iron the laundry," Mrs. Clark explained.

Jewel thought this would be a good place for her to start working. She was close to Victoria and Mrs. Clark seemed nice, but she was sure only time would tell.

Chapter 15

February 1933 arrived in Nashville with warm temperatures and heavy rain. Big Momma would say at the breakfast table, "it's too warm for this time of year, this is tornado weather." Everyone would get a laugh at her expense telling her, "You can't tell what the weather will do!" Mr. Bill would say, "The weather that's the Lord's work, let him work!" Jewel listened and smiled, she liked to walk in the rain. March had started with heavy rain and high winds; Jewel would need to change clothes when she arrived at the Clark's because she was so wet.

Mrs. Clark was setting up for a party, Saturday, March 11, 1933, and was fretting about the nasty weather. She didn't want it to affect her party. The Lord blessed her party with a warm dry day, Jewel was excited this was her first party for the Clarks. There was so much activity in the house for the party, Jewel was working late that Saturday night, to serve, and afterward she and May were to clean up. The food was extra special smoked hams, chicken, fresh fruit, cakes, pies, and special rolls that May made from scratch. There was Scotch whisky for the men and a special order of cigars was delivered. There were fresh flowers, three one hundred-pound blocks of ice were delivered, to be chopped and shaved for the drinks, and glasses frozen for the Mint Juleps.

There was a special treat for the guests, ice cream. Jewel had never seen or heard of this dessert until it was delivered. The delivery of ice cream was the last delivery made for the party, it arrived in a special truck from the local dairy, and it was boxed and surrounded by ice.

It was delivered by two colored men, one was older with gray hair, but the second man was young, tall, dark-skinned with coal-black wavy hair, his name was Craig Lee. Jewel thought he was a handsome man. After the ice cream was placed on the back porch and packed with ice, the two men came into the kitchen with small cups of the ice cream for Jewel and May to taste. The flavor was vanilla, Jewel had never tasted anything as sweet and cold as the ice cream in her life. Mrs. Clark came to check on the delivery. With her appearance, the two men went back to their truck to return to the dairy.

By 6 p.m. the guests started to arrive. Jewel was at the front door with Tim to help with the coats and hats. Dinner was to be served at 7 p.m. In the meantime, the men went to the study for Mint Juleps while the ladies inspected the parlor and talked.

Tim announced, "Dinner is served!" as he rang a tiny bell.

The men joined their wives and escorted them into the dining room. The table was set with white linen trimmed in gold; the room was lit by three large candelabras hanging from the ceiling over the dining room table. Jewel helped May serve the 1st course of the dinner, it was a clear broth which was followed by baked chicken, ham, vegetables, and the special rolls with hand-churned butter. Red wine was served with dinner and cool water was served to the ladies who did not drink. Dinner finished, the guests were ushered to the parlor for coffee and vanilla ice cream. The dessert was the hit of the evening; it was all the women talked about. Mrs. Clark was over the moon, her party was a success, and it would be the talk of the town. Jewel, May, and Tim cleared the dinner table and removed the dishes from the parlor.

Mrs. Clark came into the kitchen before she joined her husband upstairs. "You may take any leftovers home. You may also take the leftover ice cream," Mrs. Clark told the women.

Jewel told May, "I can't wait to see Victoria's face when she eats the cool treat."

It was midnight by the time everything was clean and put away. Jewel was happy she was to be off Sunday and so was May, they giggled and talked as they walked back to the boarding house. May bid Jewel goodnight, as she went to Big Momma's room to get Victoria. Both had fallen asleep, she picked up the baby and did not disturb Big Momma. When she was in her room, she unwrapped the ice cream and scooped up some on her finger, Victoria cooed and smiled she grabbed at her mother's finger for more, she loved her first taste of ice cream. Monday was the beginning of Jewels' workweek. As she walked to work, she felt the warm air on her face as the clouds hide the sun, she was happy it was warm and dry for her walk to work. Tim and May were in the kitchen talking to Mrs. Clark when Jewel arrived.

"I wanted to show my appreciation for the good job you did on Saturday, and I have a shiny dollar for each of you," Jewel and May sang as they danced around the kitchen with their dollars.

The next day Tuesday, March 14, 1933, the temperature that morning was 70 degrees. "It is too warm for this time of year; this is Tornado weather!" Big Momma said.

Everyone at the breakfast table smiled as they looked at one another. Jewel enjoyed the warm breeze as she walked to work but felt uneasy, she started to remember Big Momma's talk about tornadoes.

Jewel went about her daily chores at the Clark home. As she worked in the yard beating the parlor rugs, she noticed the thermometer on the side of the house read 80 degrees. It seemed to be a perfect spring day until it started to rain. The rain increased with high winds, the sky was almost black, Jewel and May were scared. Jewel was worried about Victoria, she wanted to go home.

"Mrs. Clark, may I leave? I want to go home to my daughter before the weather gets any worse."

"I understand as a mother I would want to know my child was safe," Mrs. Clark replied, "leave."

The rain came down harder and harder as Jewel walked to the boarding house, it was hard to see where she was going. To get her bearings she stopped in the doorway of a store, while she was there the awning blew off, she decided to keep moving, she had to get to Victoria. The streets had started to fill with water, it was up to her knees by the time she saw the boarding house. She was in a panic. She tried to run but the water weighed her down. Jewel reached the front door of the boarding house; it had been blown away and there was water everywhere.

"Big Momma! Big Momma, where are you?" Jewel started calling.

She heard her call from the top of the stairs, she had Victoria in her arms. Jewel ran up the steps and took the baby from Big Momma.

"We've got to get out of the house, it's flooding there is water everywhere!" shouted Jewel.

Big Momma just froze, she could not swim and was afraid she would drown in the high water. "We can ride the storm out in the attic, the water won't rise that high!"

Jewel looked at the scared woman, whom she had come to love, she did not want to leave her all alone. She held Victoria close to her breast and climbed the ladder to the attic with Big Momma. While in the attic Jewel found a trunk that was filled with blankets, she removed the wet clothes from Victoria and wrapped her in the dry blankets. Big Momma could not be consoled, she rocked back and forth praying. Jewel wrapped a blanket around her shoulders. Jewel then looked out the attic window as Big Momma screamed for her to get away from the window. It's a tornado, she heard a train, which is the sound a tornado makes when it is close. At that moment Jewel could see the funnel cloud, as the wind beat the walls they started to shake. Big Momma pulled Jewel and Victoria to the floor as she covered them with her body, the roof of the attic was ripped off.

They were now being hit with heavy rain as the wind got stronger and louder. The roof gave way as the tornado sucked Big Momma out the room, the floor collapsed, Jewel and Victoria were dropped into water that was up to Jewel's waist. She was struggling to keep her footing and hold onto Victoria at the same time. She was being pulled down as she prayed for God to give her strength to stay above the water and hold onto her baby girl. The floodwater started to pull her down and she felt Victoria slip out of her arms. She was in a panic when out of nowhere, a strong arm reached down and lifted her up, it was Craig. He had Victoria in his left arm and lifted Jewel up with his right. He pulled her out of the dark water and was able to wade through the floodwater with Jewel and her baby girl. The rain had stopped, and the winds started to calm as Craig walked through the floodwater. He reached a house that had not been damaged by the wind and flood water, he laid Jewel on the porch with Victoria in her arms she passed out.

Chapter 16

Jewel awoke to a roaring fire in the hearth of the house where Craig had sought refuge from the storm. She looked around the room and went into an immediate panic when she realized she was in the room alone. She was wrapped in blankets as her wet clothes dripped by the fire. She gathered her thoughts and wrapped the blanket around her, she went to look for Victoria. As she walked down the hall, she heard an unfamiliar male voice humming a tune, maybe this was his house? As her eyes adjusted to the light, she saw Craig holding Victoria, feeding her from a bottle. Craig looked up and saw her standing in the candlelight, he thought she looked like a queen wrapped in the blanket.

"Your baby girl has been looking for her mother," Craig said

She approached Craig and picked up her daughter, she started to cry from relief, she was sure Victoria had been lost in the floodwaters. She said, "Thank you for saving us from the flood. You saved both our lives."

Craig told her, "I had gone to Big Momma's house looking for you when the sky started to get dark. I wanted to make sure you were okay. Big Momma told me you had not gotten home from work, and she was watching the baby. She was worried and asked me to go look for you. I must have just missed you. When I got to the big house, Tim told me you were on your way home. That's when I came back to Big Mommas. I saw the roof fly away as I came in the house."

Jewel said in a sad voice, "Big Momma saved me and Victoria. She covered us with her body, and she was sucked out of the attic when the roof flew off."

Craig pulled her to his chest, hugged her and the baby, he said, "From this day forward, I will be here to protect you and Victoria."

The storm and flood had taken a toll on Nashville and its residents. There were many lives lost along with major property damage. Big Momma's house was washed away, and Jewel was never to see any of her boarders again. The dairy where Craig worked was in South Nashville, it suffered some wind damage, but it was still standing, which was a blessing for Craig, he was able to keep his job.

"I want us to move closer to my job in South Nashville," Craig said.

Jewel thought about this and was unsure how to answer him. He saw the confusion on Jewel's face and said, "Will you marry me?"

Craig had gotten down on one knee, proposed, and gave her a small gold band. Jewel and Victoria owed him their lives, she thought. She cared for Craig, but she was still in love with Victor. She was an honest person, she told Craig, "I want you to understand, I don't love you as a wife should love her husband."

He looked hurt and said, "I love you and Victoria, I want to make a family with you, and I know in time you will come to love me as much as I love you."

Jewel smiled, she said, "Yes."

Craig and Jewel were married by the local Justice of the Peace, Monday, May 1, 1933, and with two little words of I Do, her life changed. She was now a wife and mother, no longer living in sin, it felt good. Craig had no automobile and walked to and from work; he didn't work on Sundays. He found a nice little house for them to live, it was a 20-minute walk to the dairy.

The house had a front room, kitchen, one large bedroom with a sitting room that was perfect for Victoria's room. A small back porch where she could sit and enjoy the sunshine with Victoria. There were flowers blooming in the yard along with a big shade tree and best of all there was indoor plumbing, no more outhouse. Jewel went about decorating the house, with bright yellow curtains at the front room window, red and white checked curtains for the kitchen. She made curtains for the bedroom with dark fabric to block the sun as Craig worked different shifts and sometimes slept during the day. This also made the room quiet for Victoria's nap.

Mother Ida heard about the flood and decided she'd visit Jewel, her new husband, and granddaughter. She was driven to Nashville by Mr. Casey. The truck was filled with linens, baby clothes, dishes, a new crib for Victoria, vegetables, and smoked meats. Jewel was happy to see her mother and hear the latest news from Allen. As Mother Ida helped unload the truck Jewel asked, "Is Victor still in Allen or has he moved back up North?"

Mother was shocked to hear her ask about Victor. Mother Ida said, "Girl, why are asking about Victor? I thought you were over him; you are married! "

Jewel looked at her mother and said," I don't love Craig. I told him so when he proposed."

Mother Ida was stunned at the revelation from her daughter. "When we get the truck unloaded, we need to have a long talk," Mother Ida said.

When everything from the truck was put in its proper place, Mr. Casey made a little spot next to the fire to sleep. Jewel made tea for herself and her mother. Mother Ida played with Victoria as she watched her daughter. When the tea was ready, she sliced the cake Sadie made and the two women started to talk.

Mother Ida said, "So, you say you don't love Craig even though he saved you and Victoria?"

"Yes," Jewel said.

"Have you consummated your marriage?"

"No," Jewel said.

"I see you have followed in my footsteps. Marrying a man that you don't love."

Jewel looked up from her tea as she realized what she had done. "I care for Craig. He loves Victoria, and he has been very patient not demanding to consummate the marriage. He seems to understand what I am feeling."

Mother Ida shook her head, "Don't wait too long to be a real wife to him, he's patient now but who knows how much longer that will last." "I destroyed a wonderful man who loved me, I just could not return his love, we are married in name only that is an awful way to live."

"I live that way because I have no place to go and to start over at my age would be hard. Jewel you are young, and you have your whole life ahead of you. If this man loves you and your child, open your heart to him, let yourself heal. The only way that will happen is for you to let Victor go. I know it's hard, but you have a good husband, don't lose him over a man who is not worth the salt in his bread."

The mother and daughter finished their tea in silence. Jewel knew she was not honoring her husband as God had commanded. Victoria started to cry at the same time Craig came home from work. He picked her up to comfort her before her mother could reach her from the kitchen. Mother observed this with major interest, she smiled when Victoria was placed in her arms. Craig had never met his mother-in-law and was very polite and respectful. Craig introduced himself as Mother Ida continued to watch the interaction between her daughter and her husband.

Jewel made dinner for them, Mr. Casey was happy to wake up and have dinner, he had not eaten much on the road to Nashville. Craig always had a good appetite and seemed to enjoy the meals Jewel made.

Once everyone was seated around the table, Craig blessed the food, "Lord thank you for the blessings you have given to me, my wife and beautiful baby girl. This wonderful meal and Lord please look over my mother-in-law and her driver as they travel home. These blessings I ask in your name."

Everyone said, "Amen."

After dinner, everyone went to the front room for coffee and cake.

Mother Ida asked, "Will you let me take the baby to Allen for a few weeks?"

Jewel almost chocked on her cake; she was not expecting that question. Victoria was 20 months old; she had never been away from Jewel no more than a few hours at a time, and that was when she was working. Jewel could not speak, she got up from the sofa and took the cups, plates, and cake to the kitchen. Once she was in the kitchen Mother Ida asked Craig, "How do you feel about me taking Victoria home with me? You and Jewel are newlyweds, I think you need some time together without the presence of a baby."

Craig was stunned he knew how protective Jewel was of Victoria, he said, "Whatever Jewel wants to do is ok with me."

Mother Ida walked to the kitchen and watched her daughter cleanup she was in a frenzy. Mother Ida asked, "Is there something wrong?"

"Wrong!" Jewel screamed, "You want to take Victoria to Allen! Why would you want to take my baby away?!"

Mother Ida said, "Calm down let's sit and talk."

Jewel and Mother Ida sat down she explained, "I want to take Victoria to Allen for one reason only and that is to give you some time with your husband, alone. It's obvious he loves you and Victoria; you owe that time to your new husband and yourself."

Jewel sat in silence for what seemed hours when she said, "You are right. I do owe my husband some time without the baby. If you take her, I want her returned to Nashville after the 4th of July."

Mother Ida agreed, it was the end of May, Victoria would be gone about six weeks. Jewel and Mother Ida returned to the front room, where she said, "Craig, I am going to let my mother keep Victoria until the 4th of July. Do you agree with my decision?"

Craig said, "Yes, whatever you want."

The next morning was full of activity getting Victoria ready for her trip to Allen. It was a beautiful sunny day, the trunk with baby clothes and diapers was loaded onto the buggy. Jewel kissed Victoria on her fat little cheek as she handed her to Craig who also gave her a kiss as he handed her to Mother Ida. Victoria was looking back as the truck rolled out of sight. Jewel looked at Craig, they smiled at each other as they walked back into the house.

Chapter 17

A beautiful warm sunny day greeted Jewel as she prepared breakfast for herself and her husband, it seemed odd to Jewel that she was not making baby food. Craig smelled the fresh coffee, bacon, and biscuits baking as he shaved for Church. He came to the breakfast table where a hot plate was waiting for him, he gave Jewel a kiss on the back of her neck as she stood over the stove. Jewel made her plate and joined her husband; he blessed the food. After the breakfast dishes were cleaned, and things put away both Jewel and Craig got ready for Church.

This was a special Sunday; the adult choir was singing, and Jewel had a solo. When it came time for her to sing, the church was quiet; once she finished singing the church erupted in claps of joy. Craig was so proud of his wife he could hardly keep still in his pew. The sermon for the day struck home for both Jewel and Craig, as it was about husbands and wives, Jewel listened intensely she wanted to honor her husband. When church service was over, there was a fellowship dinner sponsored by the Mother Board. They made a wonderful spread of fried chicken, ham, rolls, fresh vegetables, and pies. There was sweet tea and lemonade served as everyone made their plates.

Mother Sue asked Jewel, "Where is Victoria this fine day? I hope she's not sick. She is always with you and your husband for Sunday Service."

Jewel replied, "She is fine. She is spending a few weeks with her grandmother."

Mother Sue smiled and said, "I bet your husband is looking forward to having some alone time with you, after all, you are still newlyweds!"

Jewel looked at her and smiled, just as Craig walked up. Mother Sue winked at him and walked away.

Craig asked, "Why is Mother Sue winking at me?"

"She was winking at you because Victoria is gone, and we are still newlyweds."

Craig laughed, "Those little old ladies are in everybody's business!"

Jewel laughed along with her husband when she stopped and kissed him sweetly on the lips. Craig was not expecting a kiss and looked like the little boy whose hand was stuck in the cookie jar, Jewel laughed at the look on his face. After eating and talking with other church members, Craig was anxious to get home and be alone with Jewel. Was today the day he and Jewel will consummate their marriage, he thought. They walked home holding hands, not speaking but smiling at each other as they walked. It was late afternoon by the time they got home, the sun was just making its way across the summer sky as the cool evening breeze began to blow.

Once home, Craig prepared a hot bath for Jewel, as he watched her undress, he could feel the excitement wash over his body. Jewel could see Craig was excited this made her feel shy and awkward, as he held out his hand to help her get in the tub. Once in the tub, the warm water started to relax her body. It felt good especially when Craig started to wash and massage her back. As the heat of the water started to cool, Jewel could feel her passion for Craig rise as he massaged and washed her breast. The feelings she was having were not close to what she felt that one night she was with Victor. Jewel thought "This is what it must feel like when a man loves you, he takes his time and considers your feelings." Jewel closed her eyes leaned back in the water as Craig touched her thigh. When he touched her "special place" she moaned "Don't Stop."

He leaned in and gave her a warm wet kiss, he then helped her out of the tub, wrapped her in a towel, and carried her to their bed. The passion that ran through Jewel's body scared her, she said to Craig, "I want you to know, you are the only man to make me feel this way. I never felt this way with Victoria's father. I'm not sure what I should do. I don't want to disappoint you."

Craig gave her another warm kiss and said, "I understand everything you are feeling, I love you. I want you to feel my love, just let me show you."

Craig started to kiss Jewel's neck as his hands stroked her breast, he kissed her nipples, and she started to tremble with anticipation. He then turned her over onto her stomach, spread her legs, and continued to touch and caress her. Just when she thought she was going to faint from the passion, Craig wrapped his arm around her waist, pulled her bottom up and close to his member. With a long smooth stroke, he entered Jewel. At that point, instinct kicked in and she started to move her body in rhythm with his. The release came with a moan from Jewel and a sigh of relief from Craig. Jewel rolled over to her back as Craig moved to hold her in his arms. I am laying in my husband's arms, she thought with a smile. He kissed the back of her neck as they fell asleep.

Monday morning dawned with Jewel waking early and sitting in the chair across from the bed watching her husband sleep. She watched his chest rise and fall under the sheets, she could see the outline of his manhood, and she smiled as it seemed to move on its own. She thought I have been blessed, I have a loving husband a beautiful baby girl and a home of my own. She gave her husband a light kiss on his cheek and went to the kitchen to start breakfast.

It was 6 a.m. Craig had to start work in an hour. She went to wake him with a cup of coffee. She called his name and he stirred, she turned to put the cup on the side table when Craig caught her by surprise. He grabbed her and pulled her onto the bed. He kissed and tickled her neck at the same time. In the middle of laughing, she said, "Stop I can't stand to be tickled."

But he continued to tickle her, and she continued to wiggle and laugh. He finally stopped when he noticed the time. "I better get going or I'll be late for work," he said.

Jewel ran to the kitchen and packed his breakfast; two sausage biscuits and two ham sandwiches for lunch. He washed, dressed, grabbed his lunch bag kissed Jewel and he was out the door. Once Craig was out the door, she was able to get started with her chores. She washed clothes and hung them on the line out back to dry. She let up all the windows in the house for the fresh air to come in the house and she started dinner. She decided to make chicken and dumplings, the same recipe she was taught when she lived on the farm with Grandmother Lizzie. Now she was glad she had learned to cook at an early age.

The sun had started to set when Craig came into the house from work. He picked Jewel up and danced around the kitchen; he kissed her, it was wet and warm. Craig put her down and went to wash up for dinner as Jewel set the table with candles, plates, and spoons. Once Craig came to the table, she served her husband, his plate was filled with the chicken and dumplings alongside was cornbread and buttermilk to drink.

Craig said, "That was wonderful, I feel like a king!"

Jewel cleaned the kitchen and put all the things away as Craig sat on the back porch smoking his pipe enjoying the cool breeze. Jewel joined him and sat in the opposite chair.

"This has been a wonderful day but it's better now that you are home," she said.

Craig looked at his wife and smiled. He put down his pipe walked over to Jewel picked her up and walked up to their bedroom. She sat on the side of the bed as she watched her husband undress. His dark brown skin looked like marble in the candlelight, the muscles in his stomach were tight, his thighs and legs were muscled and strong. She was proud of her husband and his body. While he lay in the bed waiting for Jewel, she took off her clothes and splashed her body with the special toilet water she had received from Mother Ida, Craig loved it. When she climbed into bed, Craig began to kiss her lips and neck, she rolled him over to straddle his dark strong body. He relaxed and let her take the lead, she sat on his chest and rubbed her body up and down his chest. She kissed his neck; she could feel his manhood rise and beg for attention. This made Jewel more aggressive, she pulled herself to her knees and lowered her body onto his member. They both started to move in rhythm. Soon the dance ended with Jewel collapsing onto Craig's chest. As she stretched her legs out, she felt him slip out of her and the warm liquid from his body run down her leg, she smiled.

    He held her close and said, "I love you"

    Unexpectedly she replied, "I love you too."

    Craig could hardly believe his ears. His heart leaped in his chest he fell asleep with his love in his arms.

Chapter 18

Jewel had settled into a wonderful life with Craig and Victoria; she had been married for five wonderful years. Today was extra special it was Victoria's birthday 5 years old.

It was a beautiful crisp October day, Mother Ida and Father were coming to Nashville for Victoria's birthday celebration. Victoria was growing into a beautiful little girl who was curious and smart as a whip. Jewel had been so busy getting things ready for the visit from her parents and the party, she didn't think about her morning sickness and not being able to keep any food down. Jewel decided to see her neighbor Miss Tammy; she was the local midwife. She also made salves and medicine from the herbs she planted in her backyard; everyone went to her when they were sick.

Jewel said to Miss Tammy, "I have been so tired and sick these last few mornings, I'm sure it's just the excitement of Victoria's birthday party."

Miss Tammy looked at her and said, "Honey, it's not the birthday party. You are going to have a baby!"

"What?" Jewel exclaimed. "How can you tell by just looking at me?"

"Tell me, have you had your monthly bleed?"

Jewel thought and said, "I really paid it no mind because I have always missed months."

"Looking at your eyes and the little belly you have, I will say you are about three months gone," Miss Tammy said.

Jewel looked down and patted her belly, she smiled. Craig will be so happy, Jewel thought. I have been blessed with another baby, I will ask Father to look at me to make sure, and then I will tell Craig after Victoria's party.

The family from Allen arrived and it was a joyful day. Father and Mother Ida had gifts for Victoria wrapped with shiny paper and bows. She also brought jams, fresh-baked bread, and smoked meats.

Father gave Victoria a hug and looked down at her belly saying, "Jewel, honey, are you going to have another baby?"

"I might be according to the midwife next door. Can you tell for sure?" Jewel asked.

"Yes," Father replied

"Let's get everything unloaded and into the house," Jewel said.

Victoria was happy to see her grandparents. She ran to the door to give them both big hugs and kisses. Mother Ida got down on her knees and gave her a big hug.

"Oh my, you are such a big girl!" Mother Ida said as she looked at Jewel.

Victoria ran to Father who picked her up and danced around the room with her.

Mother Ida said, "She looks more like her father every day."

Jewel looked at her with a frown and said, "She only knows Craig as her father. Please don't bring up the Cotton family in this house. That part of my life is over, I am happy with Craig. He is a wonderful husband and father; I don't want him upset or Victoria confused."

Mother Ida looked at her daughter and was proud of her, she had made a new life and was happy. "I am sorry I brought it up. You are right, Craig is Victoria's father."

The two women smiled as they watched Father play with Victoria. The sun was going down and Craig would be home soon; time to get dinner on the table. At 6 p.m. Craig walked into the house and was greeted by Mother Ida and Father. He then lifted Victoria and gave her a big hug and kiss on her cheek saying, "How is the birthday girl?"

Victoria laughed and said, "Happy I want cake!"

"We can have cake after dinner."

She smiled as he put her down, she ran to the kitchen. "Daddy's home," Victoria said with a big smile. "We are ready to eat cake!"

Jewel left the kitchen to greet her husband with a sweet kiss and hug. She was so happy to have all the people she loved together. Mother Ida was making the table look grand with a white tablecloth and fresh greens from the yard to add some color to the table. The room smelled like Christmas; the special birthday dinner also made it seem like Christmas.

Everyone was seated around the table and Craig made a wonderful fire in the hearth. Father prayed over the food and Jewel had a feeling of contentment she had never known before. Her life was good with many blessings. Dinner was over, it was time for the birthday cake and ice cream. Everyone sang happy birthday and Victoria blew out her five candles, she had cake all over her face, all the adults laughed. After the kitchen had been cleaned, it was bedtime for Victoria. After a bath she was put to bed with her new doll she named Polly. With kisses from all, she fell asleep.

Mother Ida wanted an after-dinner walk, Father said, "Craig, will you walk with my wife tonight? My knee is stiff tonight and I just want to put it up on a stool."

Craig said, "I'd be happy to walk with Mother Ida. We will be back directly." He gave Jewel a kiss on the cheek, he and Mother Ida were out the door.

"Jewel let's take this time to see if you are really pregnant." After the exam, Father confirmed what Miss Tammy said, she was indeed three months pregnant. "How do you feel about this new life?"

Jewel smiled, "I am over the moon. This will make Craig so happy. I can't wait to tell him."

Mother Ida and Craig returned to hot coffee and birthday cake. There was news from Allen, but the only thing Jewel could think about was her baby news. Father yawned, "Time to turn in Ida, we have a long ride tomorrow." They were sleeping downstairs on the sofa and loveseat.

Jewel prepared a hot bath for her husband and washed his back. He leaned back into the tub as the warm water splashed on his dark-toned body. Jewel was able to see her husband become aroused as she washed his thighs. She stepped back from the tub and dropped her dress, she stood in the candlelight as Craig got up from the tub. He smiled as she wrapped a towel around his waist. A chill went through her as she watched him dry his body; she could feel herself become aroused. It felt like the first time they were together. Craig could always arouse her, and he knew it as he watched her nipples stand up. He walked over and gave each nipple a sweet kiss. He ran his hand up her thigh and could tell by the way she moaned she wanted to feel him inside her.

He dropped his towel picked Jewel up and walked toward their bed, he laid her down as he kissed her neck and down her breast. She ran her fingers down his back, she relaxed and felt his thick, firm manhood enter her. She thought she would pass out when he entered her and started to move his hips in rhythm with hers. It was soon followed by the sweet release they both wanted, Jewel moaned, and Craig's body started to shake, it was wonderful. As Craig rolled to her side, Jewel moved her leg over his hip and gently kissed his neck. She ran her hand over his strong chest and down his stomach, she felt his stomach quiver.

"Jewel, I love you."

Jewel replied, "I love you so much and so do our babies."

"Babies?" He said.

"Yes," she said, "Victoria and our new baby. We are due in the Spring."

Craig sat up in the bed as Jewel laid back on the pillow. "Are you sure?"

"Yes," she replied, "Father told me for sure while you were out walking with Mother."

Tears filled Craig's eyes as he got out of bed and fell to his knees thanking God for his family and the new life they had made. He brought warm water and a cloth, to the bed, and washed her thighs. Afterward, he got back into bed, kissed her, and fell asleep with his hand on her little round belly.

Chapter 19

It was May, according to Father the baby was due toward the end of the month. He would not be there for the birth, but he told Jewel Miss Tammy would be able to deliver her baby with no problems. The month of May started off very hot and the heat made Jewel sick, she was unable to keep food down and she had constant dizzy spells. She had taken to her bed; Mother Ida had come in from Allen to take care of her and Victoria. Craig was very concerned by her sickness, he could see she was losing weight, and knowing she was sick bothered him. He felt responsible.

"Jewel, I love you and would have never wanted to see you this sick, I am sorry to have asked for another baby. I should have been satisfied with your love and Victoria."

Jewel replied, "Having your baby was in God's plan for us, he will bless us with a beautiful healthy baby boy."

She stroked his head as he got down on his knees and laid his head on her very pregnant belly. "I can feel the baby move and kick, does that hurt?"

Jewel replied, "No."

Craig stood up and said, "Get some rest, I will help Mother Ida with Victoria, so she can get dinner ready."

As he left the room, Jewel placed her hands on her belly and said to the baby, "Your daddy is worried about us. I think it's time you get here and put his mind at ease."

Mother Ida made Jewel a tray that Craig took into the bedroom. Jewel sat up in bed while she ate, Craig watched her eat, he didn't speak, and Jewel could see he was worried. After dinner, Mother Ida said, "It's a beautiful evening, you need to get out of bed for a while. You and Craig should take a short walk."

Jewel agreed, she and Craig walked out in the backyard and looked at the new flowers that had started to bloom. Holding her hand, they walked very slowly. After their walk, Craig helped Jewel with her bath. He brushed her long dark hair and helped her put on her nightgown. Craig got a bath and slipped into bed, Jewel was fast asleep, he gave her a sweet kiss on her cheek and laid his hand on her belly and fell asleep.

Sunday morning, May 20, 1938, was beautiful and sunny. Jewel was watching her husband sleep when her water broke. She could feel the labor pains start, she shook Craig and said, "My water broke, I need you to go next door and get Miss Tammy."

Craig jumped up and started to run out of the room. Jewel laughed, "Baby you need to put on some pants, I'm sure Miss Tammy does not want to see you in your underwear!"

Craig laughed put on his pants, woke Mother Ida, and ran next door. He knocked on her door shouting, "Hurry Jewel's water broke!"

Miss Tammy came to the door and said, "Calm down, let me get dressed. I will be over directly!"

Craig returned home, Mother Ida was boiling water and getting clean towels, sheets, and the baby blanket that was made just for the new baby. Victoria was sitting in the middle of the floor in the front room when Miss Tammy arrived, "Mommy is having a baby, I'm a big sister!"

Miss Tammy smiled and walked into the bedroom where Jewel was in full labor. Miss Tammy went to work making her more comfortable and gave her some herbal tea to drink to help with the pain. Craig was pacing in the backyard; he could hear the muffled screams of pain from his wife.

Then suddenly there was a hush that went over the house, Craig peeked in the back door, Mother Ida said, "Come on in."

As he stepped into the kitchen, she said, "Go to the bedroom see Jewel and your new baby."

Craig walked into the bedroom and Jewel smiled and said, "Come and meet your son."

Tears started to run down his cheeks when he looked at his son for the first time. "His name will be Adam; he is my first son."

Jewel smiled as he held his son and walked around the room. She now knew what it meant to have a wonderful husband to share in the birth of a child, she thanked God for Craig and her beautiful baby boy, Adam.

Adam was now a month old, he had fat little cheeks and a full head of hair from birth, his complexion was the color of coffee with milk, he had large black eyes that seemed to look thru to your soul; he was the apple of his mother's eye.

Victoria was taking her duties as a big sister very seriously helping with the baby. She helped with the feeding, changing diapers, and keeping him entertained as their mother went about her day. Craig was a wonderful father; he would get up for Adam's early morning feedings and change diapers. Adam was thriving, Victoria was growing up, and Jewel was happy and deeply in love with her husband.

The years passed, Victoria was ten years old and was attending the local elementary school. Adam was five years old and stayed home with his mother as Victoria went to school and his father went to work. The winter of 1943 was filled with snow and ice, Craig made a fire in the hearth for warmth and Jewel would put extra wood in the potbelly stove. The dairy was upgraded with large boilers and Craig was to clean them nightly. For them to be clean and ready for the raw milk to be delivered in the morning at 6 a.m., he would go to work at midnight and get home in time to walk Victoria to school. Because the weather was so cold, Victoria's school closed and would reopen in the spring of 1944. This decision made Jewel very happy, she would have both her babies home together. When Craig came home, he would be able to spend time with both children.

Craig came home at his usual time 6 a.m. Jewel wanted to get started on her trip to the farmers market, Craig was to be home with the children. Before Jewel left for the market, she made a fire in the potbelly stove with extra wood, kissed Adam, Victoria, and Craig goodbye. Jewel was returning home, when she started down her street, she could smell smoke, the closer she got to her house, there was more and more commotion. She saw Miss Tammy standing in the street.

"Is someone's house on fire?" she asked.

Miss Tammy looked at her with a look Jewel knew was bad she said, "What's on fire?" As Jewel looked across the street, she could see her house was on fire. She started to scream, "Victoria, Adam, and Craig" as she ran toward the burning house.

One of the firemen grabbed her and said, "You can't get through, the roof has collapsed." Jewel stood in the street, screaming, and crying until she heard Craig's voice.

"Jewel, I'm here." Craig was covered in soot and had burns to his arms and hands, he was holding Victoria, she was ok, just scared.

Jewel hugged them she asked, "Where is Adam?"

Victoria said, "Daddy tried to get Adam, but the roof fell, and he couldn't find him."

She looked at Craig's face and said, "He got out. He's a smart boy he knew to run."

Tears welled up in Craig's eyes, as he looked at the small body covered with a blanket, it was Adam, he was dead. Jewel ran over to the little boy under the blanket, he did not have a burn on him.

"How can my boy come out of a fire without being burned?"

The fireman said, "We found him under his bed, he choked from the smoke. That is what killed him, I am so sorry."

Jewel fell to her knees by the lifeless body, cried, and rocked back and forth. Craig put Victoria down and went to his wife, she buried her face in his chest and cried harder and harder, there was no way to console her. The fire was out and as the fire truck was ready to leave, a hearse arrived to take Adam to the mortuary. Jewel watched as her baby boy was lifted and put in the back of the black hearse, tears continued to roll down her cheeks.

Miss Tammy came over to her, "You and your family can come to stay with me as long as you need to."

Jewel looked at her when Craig said, "Thank you. Please take Victoria and Jewel to your house. I am going to the mortuary with Adam."

Miss Tammy walked Jewel and Victoria to her house. When they arrived, Miss Tammy started to pray as Jewel sat by the fire and held her daughter. Craig and Jewel were told the fire started in the potbelly stove and spread very quickly to the roof.

Jewel asked the fire chief, "Was it overloaded with wood?"

"No Ma'am," he replied, "there was a blockage in the pipe toward the roof. I am so very sorry for your loss."

Jewel called Mother Ida and Father with the awful news that Adam was dead. Father canceled his appointments, he and Mother Ida drove to Nashville to be with their daughter, granddaughter, and son-in-law. When Jewel saw Mother Ida, she ran to her and hugged her, both women started to cry. Father wrapped his arms around them both as he saw Craig come out of Miss Tammy's house. It was time to talk, everyone went inside, and they were given all the details of the fire and Adam's death.

"His funeral will be Saturday at the gravesite. Tonight, is the wake at the funeral home," Jewel said.

The Lee Family walked into the funeral home, Jewel and Craig looked at the sweet face of their son who looked like he was asleep. Victoria sat with Mother Ida and Father, there was silence, and deep sobs could be heard from the women who came to the wake. Jewel sat with Craig who had a blank expression, tears running and locking under her chin. The minister from church gave the eulogy, afterwards, the family and friends went to the cemetery and said their final goodbye to a sweet baby boy who died too soon.

Chapter 20

Craig, Jewel, and Victoria, moved to North Nashville in the spring of 1944. Victoria was enrolled in a new school. Craig and Jewel were able to buy a little two-bedroom house in a nice neighborhood with tree-covered streets and sidewalks. Craig bought a late model Ford Sedan, now the family had a new car and a new home, Jewel saw this all as a blessing. The church in Allen had taken up money for Jewel and her family, there were donations of clothes, furniture, and money, everyone who loved Jewel and her family helped.

The death of his only son took a grim toll on Craig, he started to drink. When he was off work, he was in a beer garden or juke joint. He would come home on payday, make sure Jewel had money to run the house, spend a few minutes with Victoria, then he was out the door until he had to go to work. The warm loving man Jewel married was gone. He was no longer God-fearing, he stopped going to church and Jewel never heard him pray. Jewel was at a loss, she loved her husband, he was so hurt by the death of Adam. He was not able to give or show love. The old saying, Time Heals All Wounds, was not always true. Time did not heal Craig. He became distant, he drank more each year, and he had his driver's license suspended after crashing his car into the side of a building.

Jewel took a job outside the home in a laundry mat, which kept her busy. She worked 12-hour days and seldom saw her husband or Victoria who was now a senior at Jones High School. Victoria threw herself into her schoolwork, she joined a girl's social club, she wanted to avoid her parents. Jewel and Craig never had a crossed word, but they were broken. Jewel worked to hide her pain and Craig drank.

High School Graduation was set for June 1, 1949, and her best friend, Juanita, who had family in Cleveland, Ohio wanted Victoria to come to her family reunion on the July 4th weekend.

Victoria asked Jewel, "Momma, for my graduation gift I would like to go with Juanita Moore to her family reunion."

Jewel didn't want her daughter to go up North, she had never spent a night away from home and now she would be gone for a week. Jewel knew the trip would be good for her, she needed to getaway. Jewel also thought if she was alone with Craig, she might be able to get back the man she lost in the winter of '43.

"Go to the family reunion and have a good time. I think a change will do you good.

"Mama," she said, "will you be all right being home alone with daddy?"

"Of course, the time will be good for us also. Maybe we can get back some of the magic we used to have before your brother died."

Victoria hugged her mother and ran next door to tell Juanita she was given permission to go with her to the family reunion. June 1st arrived with sunshine and a light breeze. Jewel looked out the window reflecting on her life. She had a beautiful daughter who was graduating from high school, the first person to do so on her side of the family. Her son had been dead for six years and his death cast a shadow over her life. Craig was still struggling with Adam's death; he could not talk about it; he was unable to touch Jewel out of fear of getting her pregnant. Jewel hoped the week Victoria was up North, she would be able to break down the barrier her husband had built.

Victoria ran into the room excited about the day and her new white dress, her cap and gown were also white; the boys were wearing red gowns. The school colors were red and white. As she danced around the room, Craig entered looked at Victoria smiled, and said, "Beautiful girl, today will be a special day you will always remember. I know I am not your natural father, but I am so proud of you, I could not love you more if you were my blood."

Victoria stopped dancing, ran to Craig's arms, and said, "I will always love and honor you as my father. Please forgive and love my mother again."

Craig said, "I love your mother. I always will but sometimes I have this darkness come over me since your brother died."

He looked at Jewel and smiled; he said, "it's time to leave for graduation."

Jewel, Craig, and Victoria left the house. Craig walked in the middle holding each woman's hand. When they arrived at the school, everyone was directed outside for the graduation ceremony. As the principal called each graduate's name, they arose from their seats, walked across the stage, to have their diploma handed to them. The Class of 1949 had 50 graduates.

Victoria wanted to go to nursing school. To help her dream come true, Jewel's mother and Father Ira were going to help pay her tuition. The Church in Allen and Nashville also collected money to donate for tuition.

Jewel was thankful for their blessings. That evening the graduates and their families were to have a party at the Church.

"Do you mind if I go to Juanita's house, she wants to talk about our trip? I will meet you and Daddy at the Church," Victoria asked.

"Yes," Jewel replied.

She watched her daughter walk out of sight and as she turned, Craig kissed her cheek.

"Ready to go home, my love?"

Jewel smiled and said, "Yes."

They walked back to their home holding hands. The sun was setting and there was a warm glow coming thru the bedroom curtains when Jewel and Craig arrived home. She walked into the room ahead of him and sat down on the bed, she motioned for him to sit; he did.

"Victoria looked so happy and grown-up today," he said.

"Yes, she did. But tell me, how are you feeling?" Jewel responded.

Craig stood up and walked to the window, pulling down the shade, he said, "I will show you."

Craig turned and took off his shirt. Jewel stood up, walked to him, and gave him a long passionate kiss. Craig removed Jewel's dress and it dropped to the floor, he kissed her neck, picked her up, and carried her to the bed. Jewel closed her eyes as Craig kissed her neck and ran his hand down her stomach to her very special spot. She arched her back and closed her things around Craig's hand and moaned. It had been years since Craig had touched her but once they dropped their defenses all their feelings rushed back. They continued to kiss Jewel helped Craig with his clothes. With their clothes on the floor, Craig rolled onto Jewel and entered her, he moaned, she was wet and warm. They still had the connection, and their bodies were in sync as they moved in rhythm, their passion peaked.

"Craig, I have missed you so much, I love you!"

Craig looked at Jewel kissing her face and neck, he pulled her close, and they fell asleep in each other's arms. When Jewel and Craig arrived at the graduation party, Victoria ran to greet them, she saw the look on her mother's face; it was continent and joy.

"I was hoping you would make it before all the punch and cake were gone" as she looked at her mother and smiled.

Craig cleared his throat and said, "I see a guy I work with, let me say hello to him and his wife."

Jewel said, "Go, I will get us some punch and cake. I will be sitting at the table by the door. I love you!" He kissed Jewel's cheek and walked over to greet his friend.

Victoria said, "Mama, are you and daddy happy again?"

"Yes," Jewel said and hugged her daughter.

Jewel looked across the room at her daughter and her friends, she looked at her husband talking with his friends from work and prayed, "My life is good, thank you Father God for my husband and daughter, I am blessed."

Chapter 21

The trip to Cleveland, Ohio, was to start bright and early on July 1, 1949. Jewel, Craig, along with Miss Tammy, went to see the girls off; they were taking a Greyhound Bus. This was exciting for both girls, they had never been on a bus. Jewel started to cry Craig pulled his wife close saying, "This is going to be a great trip for both the girls to help them be more independent."

Victoria saw her mother and daddy, "Bye everyone. I will call you when we arrive in Cleveland." There was joy and excitement in Victoria's voice.

The bus left the bus station, Craig and Jewel watched until it disappeared. Victoria and Juanita were excited as the bus drove thru three different states to their destination. Jewel had packed them a lunch of ham sandwiches and jars of sweet tea. After lunch the girls fell asleep, they were awakened as the bus made a sharp turn into the Cleveland Bus Terminal. Juanita fell off her seat and they laughed until everyone started to leave the bus. Juanita's parents, Jonathan and Esther Moore, greeted them at the bus terminal. They hugged and welcomed the girls.

Juanita hugged her parents saying, "I am so happy to be home This is Victoria, my best friend in the whole world."

Esther said, "Welcome to Cleveland and our home."

Mr. Moore picked up their bags and everyone jumped into the car and drove to the Moore family home. It was dark when they arrived, everyone took a bath and went directly to bed. The girls were awakened to fresh coffee percolating on the stove along with the smell of fresh biscuits and bacon. The girls dressed in their day clothes; they ran down the steps to the kitchen.

"Good morning girls, hope you slept well," Esther said.

"Yes, we did!" exclaimed the girls.

The girls sat down to a wonderful breakfast with fresh apple juice. After the meal, the girls helped clean up the kitchen, then were out the door to explore Cleveland. The Moore home was not in the city, so the neighbor's son offered to drive the girls around. The driver was James Smith, he was the son of Reverend Smith. The minute Victoria saw him she was smitten. James was older than Victoria, he was 25 years old. He was going to college with a major in agriculture. He was tall with curly hair his voice was deep and expressive. When he saw Victoria, everyone could see he was smitten, it was a mutual attraction. Victoria listened to all he had to say about the family farm and how he wanted to make sure the farm was producing and running well. Victoria sat in the front seat and hung on his every word.

"I have never seen James look at anyone the way he looked at you," Juanita said.

"I have never met anyone like him before," Victoria said, "he has been in school, working the farm, and has had no time for a girlfriend."

The girls laughed locked arms and ran into the house for dinner. The house was filled with relatives from all parts of the country for the family reunion and the Fourth of July. There were family members as far away as California. Everyone had babies and children of all ages. This was the first time Victoria had seen such a large family.

The men were busy digging a pit to cook a whole pig. The women were picking vegetables straight from the gardens. The smaller children were helping with the cow milking getting it in containers so it would cool. It was a beautiful sight to see how much this large family worked together and the love they had for each other.

The Fourth of July finally arrived. It was hot and there was a slight breeze a perfect day for an outside family gathering. The men attended to all the meat preparation and the woman and children set up the table and chairs underneath a large oak tree. There were neighbors who were also invited but most special to Victoria was Reverend Smith and his family. Victoria was helping with the tables when she saw James in the sunlight, her heart leaped, with joy and excitement. He walked over and took her hand.

"Hello, Victoria. I am so happy to see you, I have thought about you since our first meeting."

Victoria took his hand she smiled he helped her up from her seat. Everyone had completed their chores with all the tables set the family gathered for the blessing of the food.

Once the prayer ended and the bowls of food were passed around. Everyone laughed talked sang songs it was beautiful. After the meal, everyone pitched in to clean up the eating area it was time to bring out the wonderful desserts. There were cakes pies cookies and ice cream, by the time the desserts were finished there was a funny silence. The adults had fallen asleep along with the children. John did not fall asleep.

"Victoria, are you sleeping?"

Victoria sat up and smiled he raised her from the soft blanket and held her hand as she composed herself. This was the first time in her life she was this close to a man, it felt special. They walked he told her of his dream to make the family farm the best in Ohio. Victoria could see his dream form in her mind, she closed her eyes and could see John's success. In her imagination, she was able to see herself in his life as his wife and helpmate.

James paused, "You are so quiet; do you think this is just a dream and it's too much to hope for?"

"No, I see your dream. I understand everything you said," she replied.

He smiled they walked back to the house Reverend Smith had packed up some leftovers and was ready to go home, he called to James that he was ready to go. James squeezed Victoria's hand and then ran to his father's truck they drove away. Victoria watched until the truck was out of sight.

Juanita walked over, "I saw the way you looked at John but more important was the way he looked at you. I have not seen him for years and never saw him talk with anyone the way he talked with you. Also, the look on his face, I think he may be falling in love with you."

Victoria looked at her friend, "I hope what you saw is true because I am falling in love with him."

Juanita and Victoria smiled at each other and walked into the house. The next few days were spent exploring the farm, enjoying the great food, and resting under the oak tree thinking about what life will bring once the week was over. They were to leave on Monday.

It was Sunday, everyone put on their best and went to church. This church was Juanita's family church, people had been worshiping at this church for over 100 years. The church was set on a hill, as you drove to the church there were flowers, trees, and fruit trees. Victoria could see the Moore's family farm and the Smith's family farm it was exciting to see how close they were and how beautiful they were at a distance. The church was painted white and had a wraparound front porch. The front doors were made from a beautiful wood that was stained and glistening in the sunlight. Walking into the church, the middle aisle was made from the same beautiful wood as the door. The rows of pews were angled so no one could block your view of the pulpit. The church could hold one hundred people the way the pews were set. When you walked toward the pulpit there were beautiful tapestries and stained-glass windows, they were beautiful. Behind the minister's pulpit was the choir.

Victoria thought to herself, this is beautiful I could come here every day. I feel the presence of the Spirit and it makes me feel calm and happy. As Victoria stood in the middle of the church, she felt warm and safe. As the other family members arrived, she was able to see how close they were and how much love they brought inside the sanctuary. Juanita and her family came in they went straight to the left side of the church that was Mr. Moore's favorite seat in the church. Reverend Smith was in the back dressing in his robe with the help of James. Candles were lit once completed, the organ and piano played music for the choir to enter. The choir robes were sky blue trimmed in gold; they were beautiful the choir was fifty strong. Once the choir was in position a deacon started prayer then Reverend Smith came in and the service started.

Victoria did not notice James had come in and sat beside her. He took her gloved hand and gave it a light squeeze. This was First Sunday, there was a picnic on the lawn and fellowship. Victoria sat on the porch watching the ladies' dresses and their hats. It seemed the most popular color was yellow. Juanita's mother Esther had a beautiful sheer yellow hat with flowers on the side along with a beautiful sheer dress. Her white gloves and white sandals made her look like someone out of a movie. All the men were dressed in their summer suits of seersucker linen and cotton beautiful ties to complement their jackets and hats. The men were not considered well-dressed unless they were wearing a hat on their heads.

The Mother Board and the Usher Board were sponsoring the luncheon on the lawn. There were all kinds of food; baked chicken, ham, dressing, and macaroni-and-cheese. There were desserts cakes, pies, brownies, cookies. Fresh vegetables were placed on the tables on the lawn. The congregation was hot and looked forward to the cool drinks. The different foods, rolls, cornbread, meat, and vegetables along with dessert there was something for everyone to enjoy. Victoria stayed on the porch of the church and watched because she knew that tomorrow she would be going back to Nashville. James brought Victoria a plate of food, cookies, and sweet tea to drink. She smiled moved over and watched him sit and enjoy his meal it was great to see a man with such an appetite. As she watched John, she was sad because she knew she was going to be leaving the next day. The sparks she had felt for James were going to be left behind tomorrow morning, she was going back to Nashville.

James said, "Victoria, I have not known you for long, but I feel we have formed a special bond in the short time that we have been together. I don't know if you feel the same way, but I want to stay in touch."

Victoria smiled, "I am so impressed with your plan to make your family's farm prosperous for the future. However, I have plans to go to nursing school once I return to Nashville. My family, my church, friends, and neighbors all have contributed money to my education. I can't let them down. This is something that I have looked forward to since I was a little girl. I want to keep in touch with you but I don't want to lead you on. I don't think Cleveland, Ohio, is the place for me."

James looked into Victoria's eyes and understood exactly what she meant. Victoria was a girl with a plan, she was not going to be deterred, James was proud of her. He smiled, stood up, and gave her a sweet kiss on her cheek. He walked away from the church; she never saw him again. He did not come to say goodbye before the bus left for Nashville. There were friends and relatives to say goodbye. It was a sad goodbye for Victoria, she knew she would never see these special people again.

Chapter 22

Once the bus entered the terminal in Nashville, the girls woke up and started to gather their things. Juanita looked out the window she saw Victoria's parents and Miss Tammy everyone was so happy to see them once they got off the bus. The first thing Jewel wanted to do was feed the girls, but they had been on such a long ride, all they wanted to do was sleep. They decided they would get together for dinner the next day. Victoria woke up in her own bed it seemed that the last week was a dream, but she was happy to be home. She washed her face put on her robe and went downstairs to talk to her mother who was already in the middle of making dinner for the family later that evening.

"Mama, do you need any help with the preparations for dinner tonight? I am so happy to be home I didn't think that I would miss Nashville, but I did. I'll get dressed and be right down to help you."

Jewel smiled as she put the finishing touches on an apple pie. She was happy to see her daughter she prayed that Victoria would not want to stay in Ohio but come back to the people who love her, Jewel's prayers were answered. As the sun started to set jewel thought that it would be cooler to have dinner on the back patio. Craig had taken on the project with a couple of friends to build a patio in the backyard. It turned out well there was a barbecue pit, table, chairs, strings of Christmas lights, it looked like something out of a magazine. Jewel was very happy to show everyone what a wonderful job Craig had done. Dinner tonight would be the perfect time for everyone to see the new patio. Jewel and Victoria set up the tables on the new patio.

They had white tablecloths, candles for the tables, napkins that matched the tablecloth, and Jewel set the table with her wedding china. Once the tables were set and the lights turned on it was all set for the guests. The first guests to arrive were Juanita and Miss Tammy. Juanita had made special rolls for the dinner from a recipe that she got from her mother while they were in Cleveland. They were a warm golden brown and ready for the homemade butter that Miss Tammy had made. Craig welcomed the dinner guests he was proud of his home and family. He looked around the room he was blessed to have the love of a beautiful woman in Jewel and Victoria as a daughter. The food had been placed on the table it was time for everyone to be seated.

Craig looked around at his family as the ladies served the men. He thought that his life was perfect he had a woman who loved him he had a daughter who adored him he had a warm home with friends. He was also excited about the fact that he had been blessed for so many years and he wanted these blessings to continue. After everyone was served Craig stood up to bless the food. After the food had been blessed, everyone went about their business of eating and enjoying the evening. The conversation was light and happy all the guests were having a great time the food was wonderful. Dessert was served, the women sat in the backyard under the lights talking swapping secrets and telling their dreams. The men retired to the front porch where they sat having hard cider and dessert. After the women had their desserts, they went into the house to help Jewel clean up. Victoria had been preoccupied thinking about her trip to Cleveland. Jewel noticed her daughter was quiet and had a faraway look in her eyes. Victoria was happy the dinner was a success. She was happy when everyone left. Victoria told her mother good night and went to her room to prepare for bed.

Victoria was sitting in the dark looking out the window when her mother knocked.

"Victoria," Jewel said, "may I come in?"

Victoria opened the door for her mother and hugged her as she entered. Jewel asked, "You were not really with us tonight. You seemed so far away. Want to talk about what is bothering you?"

"I have been thinking about my future and what I may miss if I go to nursing school."

She told her mother about her time in Cleveland and the man she met. Jewel listened as her daughter poured out her heart, but she knew the right decision was made to return home and go to school. Victoria hugged her mother and cried. Jewel understood she was feeling happy and blessed. Her daughter's future was bright if unknown.

The lazy days of summer were winding down, days were getting shorter. Victoria was getting more excited about nursing school every day. The neighborhood was looking forward to the Labor Day block party. The party would be the last time she would have time for friends and even her family. The nursing program was 3 years, but Victoria had decided to enroll in the accelerated program which would have her graduate in 2 years. She wanted to do two years to get her degree and be able to help her family. The annual block party was a success everyone enjoyed the food and the games. Victoria looked around and felt calm, she knew her decision was right.

The party started to wind down at 8 p.m. It was Saturday and no matter how much you ate or played, everyone had to be ready for church in the morning. The teenage boys cleaned up the streets any food was given away to the different families. It was now 10 p.m. Victoria took her bath and fell into bed. She could hear her parents down the hall they were laughing talking and she knew it would soon be quiet.

The alarm went off and Victoria could smell fresh coffee and bacon along with homemade biscuits. Victoria ran down the stairs and hugged her mother and father. Today was the first Sunday so it was special. Victoria decided to wear her green sleeveless dress with a matching hat and gloves. Jewel wore her favorite yellow dress, hat, and gloves. Craig wore a summer linen suit with a yellow tie; the family was ready for church. Everyone walked to church because it was in the neighborhood, it was set on a beautiful hill surrounded by maple and oak trees. The church was white with heavy oak doors the pews were padded in heavy red cotton. Service started promptly at 11 a.m. The choir entered and sat down, and the deacons started the prayer. After the sermon, Reverend Ridley asked all members who were going to school this fall. There were ten teenagers who stood along with Victoria. The students said where they were going and what their majors would be. Reverend Ridley asked the students to come down front, they were given $50 each to use as needed. There was praise and prayer for the families who stood up to meet their children with tears, hugs, and congratulations.

Victoria was starting nursing school the following Monday, September 4, 1950.

Chapter 23

Victoria watched the sunrise from her bed with the promise of the new chapter her life would start today. Finally, the date on her calendar was here September 5, 1950. Her mother was in the kitchen making her favorite breakfast pancakes with fresh fruit. She ran across the hallway to the bathroom to take a shower. Back in her bedroom she looked at her clothes and wondered what she should wear her first day since she had not been given uniform instructions. She thought to herself, I will wear one of my church dresses in navy blue with the matching hat and her cute navy shoes. She ran down the stairs and gave her mother a big hug and kiss.

"Did you sleep well? Are you excited about your first day of nursing school?"

Victoria laughed, "You know I can fall asleep regardless of my state of mind."

Jewel made her daughter's plate and watched her eat. She thought this was the first person in the family's history that would be attending an institute of higher learning with their heads held high. No one can take away your thoughts or knowledge, she started to cry.

"Mama, what is wrong? Why are you crying?"

Jewel told her, "I'm so proud of you and what you have accomplished, and how bright your future will be."

Victoria started to cry and with both women, in tears, Craig came into the kitchen.

"What is wrong? Is this a woman thing?" he said jokingly.

The women stopped crying; both went over to Craig with one on each side hugged him and laughed. Everyone composed themselves and Jewel gave Victoria her lunch. Craig was waiting to drive her to school.

"Mama, are you coming?" Victoria asked.

"No, enjoy the ride with your father. He needs to know you are okay without me looking on," Jewel said.

Victoria smiled and jumped in the car. The day was beautiful and cool enough to let down the windows.

"Are you ready for today?" Craig asked.

"Yes," said Victoria, "I am so excited. Will you and mama be ok with the schedule and my hectic hours?"

"Your mother is very protective, but she knows you have to become your own woman. She wants you to be happy and if the nursing school does that for you, then your mother and I will make any adjustments needed."

"Victoria, you are not my natural child, and I could not love you more if you were. It has been my greatest honor to be known as your father."

Victoria smiled and took his hand in hers saying, "You are my father, my one and only. You loved me and my mama unconditionally and that means more in my eyes. God brought you into our lives and hearts and that is where you will remain, always."

Craig looked ahead as a tear ran down his face. They arrived at the Saint Agatha School of Nursing; St Agatha is the patron saint of nurses. The entrance to the school was surrounded by an iron fence. There was a young woman directing traffic who was dressed in white from her head to toe with shiny black shoes. Victoria would learn later she is a nun. The nursing school sat at the end of the street to the left of the medical school and hospital. As they drove to the nursing school, they passed dormitories, research labs, and classrooms for the medical doctors and dental school.

The driveway for the nursing students was a semi-circle so students could be dropped without cars being backed up. Victoria and Craig were amazed by the buildings and the people. Craig pulled up to drop, Victoria leaned in to kiss him on the cheek and said, "I love you."

She wanted to see him drive away but she was rushed inside by another nun. Victoria was in awe of the building for the nursing students. The hall and walls were marble that had been imported from Europe. Pictures of staff and former graduates. The lights fixtures were round globes with gold leaf accents. The hallway was filled with female and male students all trying to find their way through registration. The new nursing students were directed to a classroom with a massive blackboard that had all the new students' names. Victoria looked at the board where she found her name and seat assignment. On the desk next to beautiful windows that opened inside out was her name tag and books. She was there, everything seemed surreal. Once she took her seat, another nursing student sat next to her and introduced herself as Lisa Bell. The room was abuzz with talking and laughter. Lisa asked Victoria.

"Is this your first day of the advanced class and not a three-year student?"

Victoria explained, "No, I'm in the advanced program. I have heard it's strict and you cannot make a lot of mistakes because the teacher can at any time hold you back."

Lisa smiled, "Yes, it is strict. My sister did it, I can too."

The room got quiet when the Dean of Nursing entered the room. Her name was Dr. Ronnie Young, she got her Ph.D. in London, England, she spoke with a slight British accent. She was the Dean and told the class their instructors will be the nuns.

They all had special medical training. She started at the end of each row handing out welcome packages that had a history of the school its Mission and how it came to be.

According to the handout, thirty nuns escaped Germany during World War II, along with old-world craftsmen. The state of Tennessee gave them the land to build the facility to train Negro men and women in the medical profession. The school was nonprofit and only had limited seating for each class of nursing students. The doctors and dental students were also given the same opportunity. Victoria listened intently, she was going to be the best and at the top of her class. She felt a warm feeling in her chest as she thanked God.

The students with last name A-J would be in the same section. New friend Lisa and the other girls laughed as they were given a tour by the Nuns. The tour highlighted the nursing school classrooms, laboratories, and sleep rooms. The offices for the teaching staff and the Dean of Nursing and a small infirmity. Lisa was an out-of-town student so she was living in the dormitory; Victoria was a commuter, but she could stay over with Lisa to study if needed. Once the tour of the nursing school was over, all the students were directed to the cafeteria for a welcome lunch that was being served by the Senior class. After lunch, the tour continued with the hospital. The hospital had 5 floors. Medical patients were housed on the 2nd floor, the 3rd floor was for surgical patients along with 4 operation rooms, the 4 floor was physical therapy treatment rooms and X-ray facilities. The 5th floor was OB-GYN with 5 delivery rooms and a nursery. Victoria had not thought very much about babies until she saw the nursery. She decided at that moment she wanted to be a Post-Partum Nurse. Lisa did not get the same feeling as Victoria about babies she instead wanted to be a Surgical Nurse in the operation room. With separate goals, the two women would have some of the same classes in the beginning but when it was time to concentrate on their field of nursing, they would only see each other in passing or have lunch together.

The next tour was at the medical school. The girls were told it was off-limits to female students unless they were accompanied by a medical student, doctor, or instructor. These rules were not to be broken and if they were, you would be immediately dismissed from school with no recourse to return. Lisa and Victoria wondered why they were so strict about women inside the medical school. A fellow student told them the story of a nursing student who had jumped to her death. She had been dating a medical student for 2 years and at his graduation, he arrived with his pregnant wife. He even introduced them to each other saying the nursing student had helped him when he had a test. The student disappeared after the introduction everyone thought she had gone home instead she was on the roof. When the medical student's name was called to come on stage for his diploma, the nursing student jumped off the medical arts building. It is fair to say the medical students have a heavy workload and study schedule and will say anything to a nursing student.

Victoria thought how cruel the medical student had been. This was not going to happen to her, she was here for an education, not to play around with the medical students. The tour ended, and Victoria realized she had worn the wrong shoes. She had blisters. She had to remove her shoes returning to the nursing classroom. When she walked in with her shoes in her hands, Dr. Young looked at her as she took her seat.

"Ladies, please make sure you have the required shoes when you return tomorrow, in uniform, and ready to get to work. Improper shoes have cost many students their health. See you tomorrow at 7 a.m. Do not ask what time the class will dismiss. If you can't take these hours, then drop the program because you are already showing the administration your resolve is not for nursing," Dr. Young said.

September, October, and the 1st weeks of November passed quickly with new ideas, thoughts, and feelings. It was the last day of school until after Thanksgiving. There were students coming and going with excitement. Victoria was waiting for Craig in the cafeteria the nursing school had shut down and the staff had been dismissed. She drank hot chocolate while looking out the window. She noticed the figure of a man coming toward the cafeteria. What got her attention was the fact he was not wearing a hat on such a cold windy day. She thought if he were a male member of her family, he would have a hat with a matching scarf made by her mother.

As he came through the door, he ran his hands through his sandy brown hair. When he walked past Victoria he smiled and said, "Good evening."

Victoria smiled but before she could not speak. Craig blew his horn. As she walked to the door she looked back and noticed the handsome young man watching her leave. She also noticed her heart was beating extra hard, why? She jumped in the car with Craig, and they started to discuss the upcoming holiday. Victoria arrived home and helped her mother get dinner on the table. Jewel looked at her daughter and there was a different mood about her.

"Anything new happen at school today?"

"Why do you ask that question?"

"You have a different mood this evening like you have something on your mind."

"Yes, mama I saw a medical student today while I was waiting on daddy. I only saw him once and he spoke to me, but my heart started to beat fast. I have never had feelings like this."

Jewel laughed and pulled her daughter close and said, "Sounds like you have a crush on this medical student."

"Mama I only saw this man for five minutes, how that can be?" Victoria said.

Jewel smiled and nodded her head. All during dinner Jewel watched her daughter and said a silent prayer, God If this is the man you are sending to my daughter let him be the man Craig has been. Dinner was over, Victoria went to bed early and Jewel was having a quiet moment with Craig. She laid her head on his shoulder and told him about the man in the cafeteria. Craig smiled.

"You knew this was going to happen," Craig said.

"Yes, but not while she was in school. I don't want her to get distracted from her studies."

She closed her eyes, kissed her husband, and motioned for him to come to bed. Thanksgiving was wonderful. The family, all of Victoria's friends in the neighborhood stopped by to see her and get updates about the school. The house was filled with love and the smell of the holiday. There were dinner guests of all ages. Juanita didn't go to Cleveland, so she and Miss Tammy were invited. The table was set with one of the biggest turkeys Victoria had ever seen. Everyone was seated, Craig stood up and blessed the food. After the blessing of the food, everyone started to pass the food around the table.

Monday was the 1st day of classes to start after the holiday. Victoria was excited, she wanted to see the young man that she saw in the cafeteria before the holiday. Craig dropped her off and she gave him a quick kiss on the cheek and went into the nursing building. The nuns were there setting up for class and there were new notices on what the schedule for December was going to be. Christmas was just around the corner. Victoria collected her paperwork and sat down and started to read the notice. Christmas holiday was going to be two full weeks and she felt sad because she knew that she would not see the young man in the cafeteria for that length of time. She thought to herself why am I thinking of this man so much?

Victoria decided she was not going to bring lunch from home for the next three weeks before school was out for Christmas. She was going to take her meals in the cafeteria and look for the handsome young man that she had seen before Thanksgiving. She would go to the cafeteria between 12 and 1 p.m. looking for the young man in a very casual way. She did this for 2 weeks and never saw him during that time. Classes were winding down because it was going to be Christmas break shortly. Victoria decided that she was not going to worry about the young man any longer. Christmas was coming and a new year. For the last 2 weeks of December, there was no contact between Victoria and the young man. She never saw him. She never saw him on campus she wondered if he had dropped out. Little did she know that the handsome young man was also thinking about her, but his schedule was hectic. He was in his last year of residency and would be graduating in June and going off with his doctorate ready to practice medicine. The last day of classes finally came Victoria sat in the cafeteria in the same place she sat the first time she saw the young man.

She was waiting for Craig she was looking out the window she just sat and watched as a light snow started to fall. There were several students in and out of the cafeteria, but none were the handsome young man. Craig finally arrived; Victoria walked toward the car happy to be going home for a few days away from class. She needed to clear her head, get back on track and stay more focused on her nursing career instead of the handsome young medical student.

Christmas was always a big holiday for the family. They did not have a lot of money to buy expensive gifts, but the love, joy, food along with Fellowship at the Church all these things made Christmas special and heartfelt. Victoria would carry these memories for the remainder of her life. Craig came home with the most beautiful Christmas tree, the best one could remember from past years. Victoria and her mother trimmed the tree. The special jams and vegetables that were caned over the summer were now being brought out for the Christmas feast. The special Christmas tablecloth was placed on the table with the linen napkins. The more things that were added to the house for Christmas, the more excited Victoria became. She and her mother wrapped gifts in festive colors and placed them under the tree. It was now midnight Christmas had arrived the women were exhausted from baking and getting things ready for Christmas day.

It was 1 a.m. when Craig came downstairs looking for his wife. Victoria and her mother had fallen asleep under the Christmas tree. Craig smiled Victoria started to stir when he came downstairs. Jewel didn't move Craig picked her up in his arms and took her upstairs to bed. Victoria watches through sleepy eyes she wanted a loving man like Craig in her life. Christmas morning Victoria looked out her bedroom window and saw snow had fallen overnight, now it was really Christmas. Craig knocked softly.

"Victoria, are you awake?"

"Yes Daddy, come in."

"Your mother is still asleep. Will you help me make breakfast so your mother can rest a bit longer?"

"Of course, that is a wonderful idea. I will be down in ten minutes."

Craig and Victoria made breakfast fit for a queen. In Craig and Victoria's eyes, this was Jewel, she was their queen. Jewel was awakened to wonderful smells coming from the kitchen. She slipped on her robe to go downstairs. She was surprised that her husband and daughter had prepared breakfast. Jewel hugged them both as she sat down at the table. Victoria poured coffee for her parents and smiled as they looked at each other with such love and tenderness. Victoria decided she was going back to school and becoming more focused on her studies. She was determined to see the young medical student.

Christmas morning her parents opened gifts and some extra plates of leftover breakfast were eaten. Victoria went upstairs so her parents could exchange their gifts. She would get dressed and get things started for Christmas dinner. Victoria came downstairs and saw her parents had fallen asleep on the sofa. They looked so peaceful, again Victoria wanted a love like her parents, she would pray for God to bring her a husband.

Christmas afternoon family and friends started to arrive for dinner, gifts were exchanged. At the start of the meal, Craig blessed the family with prayer and blessings for friends and family that were here and those who had passed. Dinner was a wonderful bonding time for all.

After dinner, all the women helped clean up and packed leftovers for their homes. It was a special day for all guests and family. Victoria continued to pray for guidance and blessings as the new year arrived. School was scheduled to start the Tuesday after New Year's Day. Victoria prepared herself to return to school. She washed her uniforms and started to review books for class.

The excitement and anticipation for the new year were constant, Happy New Year January 1951.

Chapter 24

The first day back to class it was a cold windy day with ice falling instead of snow. Craig was out warming up the car, scraping the ice and snow.

Jewel asked, "Victoria, do you have everything you need for school? Do you have your lunch?"

Victoria smiled. "Yes Mama, I have my lunch. I have everything I need."

"Ok, have a good day at school," Jewel replied.

The women hugged as Victoria went to get in the car.

The ride was silent. Victoria was making plans as to how she would look for the handsome young man in the cafeteria. Craig could see his daughter was lost in thought.

"Are you ready for school? You are quiet, and you have a faraway look."

"Just trying to get my thoughts together for school," she said.

Her plan to see the young man in the cafeteria was also on her mind but she wanted to stay prayerful and talk with him before she spoke of him to her parents. Craig pulled up to the nursing school entrance Victoria said, "I love you be careful going home."

She gave Craig a quick kiss on the cheek and was out the door going into the nursing school. The classrooms were cold. The electricity had been off during the Christmas break and there would be several hours before the nursing building would be warm. Dr. Young came into the classroom for an announcement.

"Ladies, please be seated. Due to the extreme cold in the building, for the next 2 days, we will have a change in your schedule. Instead of classroom instruction, you will be given time at the hospital to explore your interests in specialty nursing such as medical, surgical, or maternity."

The room was filled with excitement. The students were finally going to see actual patients.

"When your name is called, you are expected to answer with your specialty," Dr. Young said.

When Victoria's name was called, she responded, "Maternity." After roll call, the nursing students were escorted to the hospital by several Nuns who introduced the students to the floor charge nurse. Lisa got her desired specialty, which was to work on the surgical floor and train for the operating room, they hugged goodbye.

Victoria was taken to the fifth floor where she was introduced to Mrs. Wilma Baldwin, the charge nurse. She and 2 other students who wanted to specialize in maternity care. Mrs. Baldwin showed the girls around and gave them a tour of the 5th floor. Victoria was excited, she had never seen any place like this before. When they arrived at the nursery, Mrs. Baldwin told the students that once they were gowned, they could have physical contact with the babies. Victoria was drawn to a cute little chubby face laying in her cradle.

She was not crying or making any fuss, but Victoria felt a connection with this baby and picked her up. Holding the little girl in her arms she thought, how wonderful, I would love to be a mother one day. This was a feeling that she had never had before. The students were shown to the break room. They sat there, drank juice, and discussed what they had seen so far and how excited they were to be working on the maternity ward.

About that time Mrs. Baldwin came into the break room and said, "We have a young lady that's in active labor. I want you girls to witness this."

Victoria and the other two girls walked out to the charge desk, she heard a phone call that said there is a young lady here in active labor and she will be coming to the 5th floor with her husband. We will page Doctor Rogers. The mother-to-be arrived on the floor, she was in extreme pain and her husband looked as if he had seen a ghost. She was taken into a labor room, while they were getting her settled, Victoria offered to get some juice or water for the husband. His name was Samuel Brown, and his wife was Thelma, this was their first baby. He did not know what to expect. He called his mother-in-law to let her know her daughter was in labor. No one had heard from her before they left the house.

Victoria looked at him she said, "I understand what is going on. Your wife will be just fine. Come into the waiting room with the other expectant fathers and I think that you will feel better once you talk to them."

Again, Doctor Rogers was paged, and he had not come to the floor yet. Victoria said, "Has anyone talked to the doctor? Does he realize that he has a patient?"

The nurses said, "Yes, he knows he has a patient. He is in the emergency room so I'm sure when he finishes, he will be straight up."

Mrs. Brown was in a lot of pain, she cried over and over about how much it hurt and could someone please do something about the pain. She was assured that the pain was part of the process and that once she further along in her labor, she would be given pain medication, once the baby started to crown.

Victoria offered her some ice chips and a cool cloth for her head. Mrs. Brown asked about her husband. Victoria told her he was in the waiting room with the other expected fathers and that he was doing okay.

"Mrs. Brown don't worry about your husband. He will be just fine, keep concentrating on what you need to do, and that is to deliver a beautiful healthy baby."

Thelma smiled and closed her eyes. The nurses on the floor were getting her ready for delivery and they brought in blankets, sheets, towels, baby blankets, and little baby hats because once the baby was born, they had to make sure they kept the baby warm. Just as she started to have a strong labor pain, the doctor walked through the door, and it was a total shock to Victoria. Here stood the young man from the cafeteria, in all his splendor. He was wearing a short white coat, a crisp white shirt, navy blue slacks, and white bucks. When he saw Victoria, he smiled. He got information from the labor and delivery nurse about the patient. He told Victoria she was doing a great job keeping Mrs. Brown as calm and comfortable as possible.

As her labor continued, she dilated to 9 centimeters. Dr. Rogers decided it was time to take Mrs. Brown to the delivery room. Victoria went to give her husband an update. She reassured him that his wife was doing well and that she was in delivery. She went back to observe the delivery. Victoria stood in the back of the delivery room and watched as Dr. Rogers delivered a perfect baby boy. She smiled and thought, this man was so tender but efficient delivering the baby. Victoria was falling for the man with the warm smile. She went back to the waiting room and told Mr. Brown that his wife and baby were well he could see the baby in the nursery. He thanked Victoria and walked down to the nursery to see his son.

Chapter 25

The morning arrived; Jewel had a strange feeling wash over her body. She knew this feeling was always a bad omen. She tried to shake it off and continued with her day. The morning had passed without incident but at 2 p.m., the doorbell rang. There was a special delivery letter from Mother Ida.

> *Jewel,*
> *Victor cotton was killed in a car accident in Washington D.C. in December. He was driving back to Allen to be with his parents for Christmas. The family was unable to get any information on their son, as to why he did not arrive, due to the holidays' information was unavailable. Once his parents were informed in Mid-January, they went to Washington D.C. to identify the body. Mrs. Cotton had a stroke when she saw his burned body. She was taken to a local hospital where she was in a coma for 3 days and died. Mr. Cotton took them back to his family home in Louisiana, where they were buried next to each other. Mr. Cotton closed his business in Allen, he continues to live with his family.*

Jewel was horrified as she read the letter. She dropped to her knees and prayed for their broken souls. Craig was on time with picking Victoria up from school. Jewel walked in from the kitchen and asked them both to sit down. Jewel read them the letter, Victoria started to cry and so did Jewel. Craig held the women one under each arm.

"That is a horrible way to end your life. I will pray for them."

Jewel looked at her daughter and asked if she wanted to go to Mississippi and see their graves.

Victoria said "No, I have had a hole in my heart because my family did not accept me but that holed was healed by my devoted mother and a wonderful father years ago. I am at peace about this news."

Jewel looked at her daughter and Craig together he is her father in every way. "Thank you, God. For this man, and my family."

The three said silent prayers and continued with their evening routine. There was never another conversation about the Cotton family. When Jewel thought about them, she was sad. Victor could have had a wonderful, sweet girl in his life, he decided against it. His story was repeated by many Negro men who had no idea how to love the women in their lives or raise their children. She prayed for Victoria to find a God-fearing man to help stop this curse on her community from women who just wanted love.

January and February passed, family and friends were looking forward to Spring. Victoria settled into a quiet thoughtful feeling as the weather started to warm. She continued to have thoughts about Dr. Rogers, but her schedule was keeping her busy, he was only a memory.

The first days of Spring had arrived, Victoria was ahead in her classes, she was ready for the next phase of her training. She continued to visit the cafeteria at different times, but she did not see Dr. Rogers. One afternoon, Victoria was sitting in the cafeteria next to the window, the sunshine felt good on her face. She closed her eyes and started to daydream. Suddenly, there was a tap on her shoulder. It was Dr. Rogers.

"You look so peaceful. I hope I'm not disturbing you."

Victoria smiled. "No, just enjoying the sunshine."

"I have not seen you since your assistance with the baby delivered in January. But I have been thinking about you. I wanted to talk with you."

Victoria smiled. Dr. Rogers started to talk about his family. His family home is in Atlanta, Georgia. He was a third-generation physician. His grandfather and father were also OB-GYN physicians living and practicing in Atlanta. He told Victoria his name, Asher Tobias Rogers. Victoria listened as Asher talked about his family and his goals. She could see him in her mind's eye: husband, father, and doctor.

Lunch break was over for Victoria she explained to Asher she had two classes for the day.

"Tomorrow is Saturday, will you let me take you to dinner?

Victoria smiled and accepted his dinner invitation.

"I will pick you up at your home at 7 p.m., will that be good for you?"

Victoria replied, "Yes, that will be perfect."

Victoria walked on air as she completed her classes for the day. Craig picked her up, she told him about her dinner date with Asher. She could not say enough good things about Asher, Craig smiled as he listened to his daughter. He thought, my little girl is in love and doesn't even realize

Once home, Victoria jumped out of the car and ran to her mother. She talked about Asher and wanted her help on deciding what to wear tomorrow night. Jewel looked at her daughter and smiled, this was the first time she had seen her daughter excited about a young man. She prayed if this is the man God has sent to my daughter then thy will be done. It was decided, Victoria should wear a nice black dress with a matching hat and pumps. She would look beautiful. All Saturday she thought about what the evening would bring. Finally, it was 5 p.m. Victoria started to get dressed. Her mother helped put her hair up in a way the hat would sit comfortably.

7 p.m. arrived and so did Asher, he had 12 roses for Victoria and a box of candy for Jewel. Craig opened the door and shook Asher's hand. The men exchanged greetings.

"You seem to be an honorable young man with great ambition however, this is my only child, I don't want to see her hurt. Don't play with her emotions because if you do, I promise, you will answer to me." Craig said.

Asher straightened his tie and replied, "I understand Sir. If I had a daughter, I would feel the same way. I don't plan to hurt Victoria; she is a beautiful soul."

The men shook hands just as Victoria walked down the stairs, she was beautiful. The couple said goodnight as they walked to the car, Jewel watched as Asher opened the door and helped her into the car. Craig walked toward Jewel and saw her tears, he put his arms around her shoulder.

"I know what you are thinking, he is not going to hurt Victoria, God has made that clear to me," Craig said.

Jewel smiled as they walked to the kitchen for dinner.

The restaurant Asher picked was in the heart of North Nashville on Jefferson Street. Victoria had seen the different stores, night clubs, and restaurants but never stopped. They arrived at Moonbeams, a restaurant that also had a live band and dancing. Once they pulled up, there was valet parking. The attendant opened Victoria's door and helped her out as Asher took the parking ticket. Victoria was with a handsome man in one of the area's most popular nightspots.

Asher asked, "Would you like to order, or do you want me to order for you?"

Victoria was unsure of herself. "Please order for me."

Asher ordered steak, medium-well, a house salad, and baked potatoes. He also ordered a non-alcohol wine for the meal.

While waiting for the food, Asher asked Victoria to dance. Her heart was in her throat as she said, "I don't know how to dance."

Asher smiled and took her hand, "I will show you."

The piano player sat down to play "Only You" by The Platters. The song seemed to go on forever. Asher escorted Victoria back to their table where dinner was waiting. They ate and talked about their future and the importance of family. When Asher spoke, she was lost in his smooth deep voice. His beautiful grey eyes and caramel skin were complemented by the candlelight. For the first time in her life, she was physically attracted to a man. She thought, I now understand my parents. She smiled over her glass at Asher. Asher was also under Victoria's spell. He loved her sweet voice and southern accent. He watched her eat and drink, the way she held her knife and fork were perfection to him. Asher knew women who would do anything to marry a doctor, but this was not the same feeling he was getting from Victoria, she truly was a pure soul. The evening was winding down, it was almost 11 p.m.

"It is getting late, and my will family will be going to church first thing. Do you mind if we call it a night?" Victoria asked.

Asher smiled and said, "No problem at all, I'll get your wrap."

He returned to the table, helped her with her wrap, took her hand, and led her to the front door. The valet took the ticket, and the car was brought around, Asher helped her get in.

Victoria did not have a lot to say on the way home. She was looking out the window at Nashville at night. The lights were beautiful and there were people in and out of buildings and cars up and down the street. Asher didn't talk either, he was thinking about dinner he had with Victoria and the feelings he was having. He reached over and took Victoria's hand and gave it a light squeeze, she gave him one also. They arrived at Victoria's home safe and sound, Asher stopped the car he walked around and helped Victoria to get out of the car. Asher saw her parents but pretended not to see them. The couple walked to the door. Being a gentleman, he pressed her hand and watched her turn and go into the house, she watched Asher drive away.

Victoria looked around the house, it was quiet. A small lamp was left on for her. She ran up the stairs and fell on her bed backward, she smiled and fell asleep in her dress.

Chapter 26

Jewel knocked on Victoria's door, "Are you up? Start getting ready for church."

The sun was shining bright, but it was not as bright as the sunshine she felt in her heart. Breakfast was over, everyone was dressed and off to church. Victoria sat in the back seat humming to herself. Jewel reached over and took Craig's hand, he looked over to Jewel with an assuring look and mouthed, "I love you."

There was a crowd gathering at the church, it was a beautiful spring day, everyone was there for worship and fellowship. Victoria sat with her family in their usual pew, the music started, the choir began to enter. Once the choir was set, the deacons began prayer and Reverend Ridley started to speak. Victoria tried to focus on the message, but her mind kept going back to her night with Asher. When the hymns were sung Victoria sang with new joy. There was silent prayer and Victoria prayed for guidance about Asher. Service ended there was handshaking, hugs, and enjoyment. Victoria wanted to leave, she was tired and wanted to take a nap. This was going to be a long week and she wanted to rest.

The family arrived home and Victoria and Jewel started preparing the evening meal. Jewel could see her daughter was distracted.

"Are you tired from last night" Or do you not feel well?"

"I am tired. The next few weeks are going to be busy because there will only be 8 weeks before school is out for the Summer."

Jewel shook her head and called Craig to come down for dinner. The meal was great as usual, but there was no real conversation. By the time dessert was served, Victoria could not keep her eyes open.

"Victoria, you look tired. Why don't you take an early night to get ready for school and get some sleep," Craig said?

Victoria looked at her mother, she would never disagree with Craig when it came to her, they always presented a united front. Jewel motioned for a hug and whispered, "I love you, sleep well."

Victoria ran up the steps, took a shower, dressed in her nightgown, and jumped in the bed. She was exhausted. Craig and Jewel sat on the sofa in a snuggle knot.

"Do you think this young man is going to be a problem and distract Victoria from her studies?" Jewel asked.

"I get a good feeling about him. Let them court and see where it leads," Craig said, "Are you going to be ok with her having a man in her life?"

Jewel looked at her husband and closed her eyes. She was going to pray and put it in God's hands.

Monday arrived with the brightest sunshine Victoria thought she had ever seen. To her, this was a sign from God her future was going to be bright and sunny. Craig pulled up to the school to drop Victoria. Asher was waiting, he opened the car door. He wanted to say good morning he gave Victoria a sweet smile and exchanged pleasantries with Craig. Asher walked with Victoria and asked her to meet him at 1 p.m.in the cafeteria, Victoria agreed. He kissed her cheek, and she went inside for class. Class however was the last thing on her mind. She was anxious to see Asher but afraid he may have bad news or maybe he decided he did not want to see her.

Finally, it was time to meet Asher. When she walked inside the cafeteria he was waiting and motioned her to come to join him at the table by the window. The window seat was where she first saw Asher and when they met again it was the same table, this was their table. She smiled and sat down. They had a casual conversation over lunch, but she was on edge.

Asher said, "In the time I've known you, I can only say you have become very precious to me. Meeting your family, how warm they were to me, and the way they trusted me with their daughter… I've concluded that I cannot have anyone but you in my life. How do you feel about me?"

Victoria looked at Asher and smiled. She took a deep breath, reached over the table, and took his hand. "Yes, I want you in my life." They sat at the table holding hands and smiling.

April and May were beautiful days with classes for Asher and Victoria and summer was just around the corner. The couple met every day for lunch, on the weekends the couple met for long walks, and they talked about their future. Asher had one year of residency to complete and that was also the same time Victoria was to graduate, May 31, 1952. Asher asked if he could come over and talk with her parents. He explained that his grandparents were celebrating their 50th Wedding Anniversary on June 4th in Atlanta. He wanted to take Victoria to meet his family and enjoy the weekend festivities. Starting Friday, June 8th to end Sunday. Victoria was walking on air when she got home from school. She asked her mother if Asher could come over Sunday for dinner for a serious conversation.

"Of course, dear girl. Do you want me to serve anything special?"

"Mama, anything you make will be perfect. I just have one request, will you make one of your special apple pies?"

Her mother answered, "Yes, and vanilla ice cream."

Victoria could not wait to tell Asher dinner was scheduled for Sunday at 5 p.m.

Sunday finally arrived; the family went to church. Victoria prayed her parents would not tell Asher he could not take her to Atlanta. Victoria was an adult, but she was still living at home and would never do anything to dishonor her parents. If they said no, she would be heartbroken. She also knew that if her parents said no there was a reason, they would only have her best interest at heart. Victoria was putting the final touches on the dinner table when Asher arrived, he had flowers for Victoria and her mother.

Victoria smiled and said, "These are beautiful, they will make a beautiful centerpiece for the dinner table."

The meal was perfect, roasted chicken, spring vegetables, homemade rolls with homemade butter, and of course sweet tea. The conversation was going well everyone acted as if this was something that happened every day. She was happy everyone was acting like family. After dinner ended, the men went to the back-patio area while the women cleaned up the kitchen.

Craig said, "Victoria said you had a special request, and that the dinner was to break the ice."

Asher said, "Yes Sir, I do."

Jewel walked onto the patio and asked if anyone wanted dessert, everyone said yes. Apple pie and ice cream were served under the night sky with the patio lights shining.

Once dessert was over, Asher asked if he could talk with her parents, and requested Victoria be present. Craig and Jewel were puzzled by his asking Victoria to stay. Asher began speaking of the love his family has and how traditions were very important to them. He spoke of his grandparents and the life he was living in Atlanta before he was accepted to medical school in Nashville. Craig and Jewel continued to listen. He also said his family was Catholic and was very devout the family followed all rules that were set down by the Pope in Rome, Italy. Jewel was not happy with that subject which was evident by her body language and the look on her face. She looked at Craig and he took her hand as Asher continued to speak.

"I just wanted to give you some background on my family. My grandparents will celebrate fifty years of marriage on June 4th and the family and community are set to give them a weekend of love, parties, dinner, and a special Mass on Sunday. I'd like your permission to take Victoria and present her to my family."

"So, you want our permission to take Victoria to Atlanta for the weekend?" Craig asked.

"Yes sir," said Asher.

Jewel looked at Craig with panic in her eyes. Victoria was sitting on the edge of her chair.

"Asher, you are asking a lot of us for a young man. We have only known you for a few short months. Victoria has never been out of town with someone that was not a relative, and never to Georgia. When do you plan to leave?"

"Friday, June 8th at 8 a.m. We will drive and plan to arrive by 1 p.m."

"Thank you for talking with us in person, but such a decision cannot be made without discussion."

Asher looked at the clock, "Sir it's after 8 p.m., I should leave so everyone can get some rest."

Asher shook hands with Craig, thanked Jewel for a wonderful meal, and took Victoria's hand and said goodbye. Victoria stood in the door as he drove away. In her mind, he was leaving forever. She closed the door and looked in the parlor at her parents. They had gone upstairs to their room. She decided it was time for her to get some sleep, she heard faint voices from their bedroom. She was going to pray for the best outcome.

Victoria found it hard to sleep, when the sun rose, she was sitting looking out the window. Her mother was downstairs making breakfast for the family. She decided to get dressed and go downstairs. Craig was at the table when she came down. He said good morning, but the conversation seemed forced, no one knew how to handle this situation. Jewel hugged her husband and daughter as they left for the day.

The ride to school was quiet. Victoria did not want to ask any questions, she decided to be quiet. When she was about to jump out of the car, Craig took her hand and said, "I love you."

Victoria gave him a kiss on the cheek. Victoria felt better as she walked into the nursing building. In between classes she saw Asher.

"Will you meet me for lunch in the cafeteria at our table?" Asher asked.

Victoria smiled and shook her head yes. Lunch did not seem the same when the couple came together, neither of them ate. Victoria was the first to speak of last night.

"My parents did not give me any idea what they were going to say. I will understand if you need to leave me behind and go to Atlanta."

Asher said, "It is a family obligation and family always comes first."

Victoria shook her head yes trying to hold back tears. Days passed like years but still, her parents would not discuss the trip. May 31st was the last day of school; Victoria passed all her classes and would enter her final year of nursing school in September. Asher was on track to complete his last year of residency. They were both looking forward to downtime and summer fun.

Jewel called for Victoria to come to see her on the patio. When she arrived both of her parents were waiting for her.

"Victoria, call Asher and ask him to lunch today we will give him our decision on the Atlanta trip," Craig said.

Victoria said a silent prayer, God, please let it be a good one for me and Asher. Victoria called Asher lunch was set for 2 p.m. As usual, Asher was right on time. Victoria answered the door. He looked past her since he didn't see her parents, he kissed her cheek, which made Victoria giggle.

Lunch was light as well as the conversation. Victoria had not felt this happy in days. Victoria cleared the table as her parents began to ask Asher questions about Atlanta and his family. Craig asked where they would be staying.

Asher said their family home, "Victoria will have her own bedroom and bathroom. Our family home sits on 1,000 acres, this is where all the Rogers have built their homes and lived for generations. My sister Naomi and her husband have built a home on the property. She is an attorney, and her husband Richard Dixon MD is also an OB-GYN.

My grandparents Dr. Caleb and Ruth Rogers have the bigger house that sits on a hill overlooking the one thousand acres. My father, Dr. Noah Rogers, is a founding member of the family business which is a clinic for women's health and bringing new souls into the world at the hospital.

My mother Katherine is the family coordinator. She keeps everyone on schedule for meetings, she is also the family bookkeeper. She schedules c-sections and oversees the front office of the practice and fundraisers in the community."

Craig and Jewel were amazed they had no idea our people had such deep family ties, businesses, and homes. Jewel asked about being a Catholic.

Asher said, "We believe in the Holy Trinity. The Father, the Son, and the Holy Spirit. We take communion at weddings, christenings, and days of worship. I know if you came to our church, you would feel most welcome. Catholic means community."

Jewel smiled and Victoria could now see the light at the end of the tunnel. Craig and Jewel gave Asher permission to take their daughter to Atlanta. Victoria was so relieved she started to cry and hugged her parents.

Asher said he would need to leave to make the final arrangements and have the car serviced because the trip was scheduled to start in 3 days. Asher left saying he would call with updated travel plans. Taking Victoria's hand, he softly said, "God is on our side."

Chapter 27

There was a whirlwind of activity to make sure Victoria had everything she needed to make a good impression on the Rogers family. Victoria was going to need at least three outfits for the evening parties, casual outfits, and an outfit for Sunday Mass. Jewel called on her neighbors and Revered Ridley's wife Gloria. She had assured Jewel the Catholic Faith was a beautiful religion with tradition that goes back further than slavery. Jewel was happy to learn about the way others worship God, which was extremely important to her.

    Jewel needed all her prayer soldiers to stand and give assistance to Victoria. Gloria was on the list for church clothes, Miss Tammy was making some of Victoria's older dresses into evening wear with mesh and lace, and Jewel took care of the casual day-to-day outfits. Victoria was going to accessorize each outfit with shoes, bags, hats, and gloves. The ladies all agreed that since it would be hot and humid, the outfits needed to be modest and comfortable. There were no issues with color choices since there was no actual wedding. The pastel colors were for day events and evening wear would also be a light color, no black or navy. At last, the packing was complete, and everything was set for 9 a.m. Victoria and Jewel could not sleep so they set up chairs, pillows and light blankets on the patio. This was the last night Jewel would spend Victoria for the next 3 days. She wanted to spend as much time with her as possible. The women shared sweet tea and little sandwiches. They both drifted in and out of naps and smiled and laughed as each would look at the other sleeping.

    The sun started to rise; it was a beautiful sight with drops of dew dancing on the lawn. Victoria folded the blankets and brought the chairs into the house. Victoria looked at her mother, she had an odd look on her face.

    "Mama, are you really ok with me going to Atlanta with Asher?"

    Tears welled up in her eyes, Jewel said, "Victoria, are you still my special girl? Are you still a virgin?"

    "Yes, mama," Victoria replied, "Asher would never take advantage of me like that. He cares about me. There has been no sex, just kissing and holding hands. He has never touched me in that way. As a Catholic, it's important to his faith to abstain from sex until marriage."

Jewel hugged her daughter, they both cried. Craig was standing in the doorway and heard the conversation, he smiled. 9 a.m. arrived, and so did Asher. He was greeted at the curb.

"I'm happy you are driving, with all the bags you have no room for anything else," Craig said.

Asher looked in the car trunk, "Here is my bag, it's right here."

Craig looked and laughed, "Okay son, be safe. Call us when you get to Atlanta."

He walked away to get the 4 bags Victoria had packed. She looked at Asher.

"Too much?"

Asher laughed and winked at Craig. "No sweetheart, you have the right amount."

Asher helped her into the car, Craig and Jewel watched the car drive out of sight. Craig said.

"Our little girl is on her way to becoming a woman."

Jewel smiled through her tears, "Yes."

It was a beautiful day to travel by car, a fresh breeze blew through the windows. Asher looked over and saw the contentment on Victoria's face, she smiled. They had been on the road for three hours, she suggested they take a break from driving to stretch their legs and have lunch. Asher found a shady spot to stop. Victoria laid out a blanket and set up the lunch Jewel had packed; the sweet tea was still cold. They ate, talked, and after about an hour, they got back on the road stopping at a gas station.

Asher got back in the car, "Next stop Atlanta, Georgia."

Victoria smiled, she was so excited and nervous, she wanted to make a good impression on his parents. When they crossed the state line into Georgia, Victoria noticed how the temperature changed; it was hot and humid.

Asher laughed, "Welcome to Georgia. If you're hot now, wait 'til we get into the city."

Victoria was in a quiet panic. What if her outfits were too heavy or out of fashion? She started to think of how badly this trip could give his family the wrong impression. It never occurred to her she would not know anyone; Asher would be away doing things with the family. What was she going to be doing? Will there be other unmarried women invited to this affair? She started to pray, dear Lord help me through this weekend because I need your arms around me for protection and guidance.

The Rogers family lived in the Grady Cluster of Atlanta, which were homes occupied by some of the wealthiest Negro people in Georgia. They were about five miles from the family home, it was 2 p.m. the temperature was 90 degrees, Victoria thought she would pass out. Asher could see the sweat on Victoria's face and arms, he was concerned she may have a heat-related medical issue. He pulled over to a gas station for a cold drink and to get Victoria out of the car. He got her to walk her around in the shade. God was on her side, a cool breeze started to blow, it became cloudy and there was a light rain. Victoria responded well to the drink and the cooler air.

"Asher, I think I'm able to continue, I feel better."

"Thank God," Asher said. They continued their ride to the family home.

Chapter 28

The cool breeze followed the couple to the family home. The road to the main house was paved in white pea-gravel with pink and white crepe myrtles. Weeping Willow trees were on either side of the driveway. The house on the hill looked like a house you would see in the movies. Victoria could only imagine how Asher's family would react to a country girl from Tennessee.

He started to tell Victoria about the different homes and parts of the property.

"There is a family cemetery and mausoleum on the property, this is where all my ancestors are buried. The family was given 1,000 acres when General William Sherman swept through Georgia. He was quartered at the plantation manor house. Before he left Georgia, he freed the slaves, he had the slave owner deed the plantation to the surviving slaves. The plantation owner was named Rogers, we took their last name. There has been bloodshed over this property, but God has helped us maintain the property and prosper."

The property had every tree Victoria had ever seen in books but the trees she loved the most were the weeping willows; they were so elegant and majestic. They drove through the main entrance passing a metal gate. Asher assured Victoria everyone was anxious to meet her. He talked to his mother and sister about the *sweet young lady* he met in Nashville. His family was not the type that let property, education, or wealth cause them to look down on anyone.

"I was taught that we are all God's children and material things were not more important than a man's soul," Asher told her.

Victoria tried to calm herself, but as everything came into focus, she understood why her parents needed so much thought about this weekend. They knew she was going into a new world; they did not want her hurt or embarrassed.

As the couple drove up, there was a welcoming committee waiting to meet Asher and his "friend" from Nashville. There were adults and children of all ages. Once Asher got out of the car the dogs ran around his legs almost knocking him down. There were hugs, kisses, and handshakes from all family members present. She had never seen so many people, so happy to have one person home for a visit. Victoria stayed in the car; she was waiting for Asher.

As she sat in the car, she looked over the house that was painted white. It was a large house with three floors. There was a wide sweeping staircase that led to the front porch. There were wide double doors that opened to the front with large pots of flowers and ferns, it was truly a southern home, not a plantation home, but a large happy home.

Asher came to the car and Victoria realized when she stepped onto his family's property her life, as she knew it, was going to change. Asher introduced Victoria to his mother and grandmother, both elegant women had swills of gray hair mixed in with their long coal-black hair. They both hugged and welcomed Victoria to their home. The teenage boys running and playing with the dogs were told to get her bags and bring them to the *Pink Room*. It was Ashton's sister Naomie's old room. The walls were a pastel pink with heavy drapes in a dark pink that matched the bedspread. She was told it got some of the best breezes at night. Since there were two Mrs. Rogers, everyone called his grandmother Grand Mere, and Asher's mother was called Lady Katherine.

The men in the house were called by their first names but no such familiarity to the women of the house. They had a position on a pedestal, and no one crossed that line. Once Victoria had gotten her composure, she was being led into the main house by Grand Mere, this was the home where it all started.

Walking into the house felt like a fairy tale. The open foyer had another grand staircase leading upstairs. To the left of the foyer, there was a library and office for the family, to the right was a formal parlor. There was a hallway next to the stairs that led to the kitchen and a formal dining room. The dining room walls were painted in gold leaf the dining table seated 20, it was beautiful. Off the backside of the house were large windows, another dining area for casual dining overlooking the backyard. The back yard was beautiful with more trees, flowers, and a beautiful green lawn, there was a back staircase used by the family to go up and down.

Victoria was led to her room which was pink and had a private bathroom, the room was beautiful. Victoria was ready to get out of her traveling clothes. The bags were already in her room, so she started to unpack, she started to feel better about the visit. She also knew she had a lot to learn, and this weekend was a test. Asher knocked on her door.

"Victoria, are you decent? I want to see you before the cookout."

Victoria opened the door and Asher entered, the first thing he did was take her into his arms and give her a hug. He explained what to expect at the barbeque. She was told to dress comfortably and that there were going to be relatives from all over the country.

"I'll see you downstairs and I will introduce you to the family," he said.

Victoria pulled a pair of slim slacks and a sleeveless shirt from her suitcase. Asher knocked; it was time to meet the family.

"Victoria, you look perfect."

The patio was lit with white lights and candles to keep the mosquitoes away. Asher introduced Victoria, the family gave her warm hugs and conversation.

There were three grills loaded with meats and vegetables. There were loaves of bread, salads, and more desserts than she had ever seen before. There was a gift table that had an attendant to keep them tidy. Once everyone had their plates, they sat down for prayer. This was the first time Victoria saw Catholics pray. Victoria loved everything about the prayer, it was beautiful. The family talked and enjoyed the meal. The remaining family members were introduced to Victoria, they loved her. They could see she was special to Asher and that made them happy. As the sun went down, the women sat on the patio talking while the men smoked cigars and drank brandy in the parlor, this was new to Victoria, she was curious.

After a while, the women started to clean up and wrap the leftovers. They were placed on the inside breakfast table. With teenage boys, eating different times they would soon be gone. The family as prominent as they were, had no outside help. The women in the family took care of the inside of the house and cooking. The men took care of the outside, vegetable and flower gardens, and the maintenance of the houses.

Naomi took the lead asking about Victoria's family and her plans for her future. The women listened as she told them about her family and friends in Nashville. The look on their faces was warm and accepting. If Asher brought her home, they knew she was special.

Saturday morning was full of anticipation and excitement for the party that night. All the meals were served, and the Champagne was given as an anniversary present by the Elder Rogers. The party for their 50th anniversary was to take place on the Rogers property in a large white tent in the back garden. There was going to be a live band with strings set near the dance floor. Tables were set with linen tablecloths and napkins with fresh flowers on the tables and silver silverware and crystal glasses. This was going to be a major milestone for the family. It was decided they would hire a caterer so the family could relax and just enjoy the party, the party was due to start at 6 p.m. that evening.

The ladies disappeared to their rooms to dress for the party, it was 4 p.m.. It was to be a formal affair the men were expected to dress in white dinner jackets, with bow ties and cummerbunds. The women of the family were expected to wear long dresses with elbow-length gloves.

Victoria was apprehensive about her dress because it was not black or navy, it was a beautiful pale yellow. She had white gloves and matching shoes. Naomi came by her room to see if she needed anything. Victoria opened her door, saw Naomi, and was immediately in tears. Naomi asked her what was wrong.

"The dress I'm going to wear will not give a good impression to the family. The last thing I want to do is embarrass Asher."

Naomi ensured her that the dress was perfect for the evening and that whatever she had to wear was going to be beautiful in his eyes because Asher had fallen head over heels in love with her.

"I will go and make sure my brother has a cummerbund and bowtie that will match your dress, this will show everyone you are a couple."

Victoria hugged Naomi before she left the room. Victoria was excited she was being invited to such an elegant affair and that the dress that she was going to wear was perfect.

Flowers were everywhere, waiters were in white coats with white gloves. There were two photographers making sure they got pictures of the guests and family. It was the most amazing thing Victoria had ever seen. It was 7 p.m., the family was arriving and so were other guests. The teenage boys were asked to park cars and make sure everyone was in a position where they could pull forward and go when the party was over. The waiters started passing champagne and appetizers. Dr. Rogers and Lady Katherine, the guests of honor, were expected to arrive and make a grand entrance. The family members were seated.

When the Rogers walked into the party, they were given a standing ovation. Lady Katherine wore a beautiful sky-blue dress, and Dr. Rogers wore a matching bowtie and cummerbund. They stopped at several tables and thanked everyone for attending their celebration, they walked to the sweetheart table that was positioned at end of the dance floor on a riser.

It was such a celebration, and Victoria enjoyed every part of it. Dinner was served in courses, which started with appetizers of smoked fish on toast points with cucumbers and dill sauce. The second course was a soup or salad, the third course was either fish or fowl. The dessert was a small chocolate pudding. A large anniversary cake was rolled into the middle of the dance floor. The couple went up to cut slices of the five-tier cake. It was the largest cake Victoria had ever seen. Each layer represented ten years of marriage. She thought how blessed she would be to find someone she could marry and stay with for fifty years. She never wanted any controversy in any of her relationships or divorce in her marriage. She was going to honor her husband and be a dutiful, faithful wife.

The cake was sliced and passed to the guests, champagne was poured and passed, and the guests and family toasted the couple. The band started playing and everyone was up to dance. It was about 10 p.m.. The night was cool, you could still feel the anticipation and excitement of the day. Victoria was happy and proud to be with Asher. She was also happy that Asher taught her how to dance. It was midnight, the family toasted to the new day, Sunday morning.

Lady Katherine announced, "Everyone will be going to mass at 8 a.m. so let's all turn in."

Everyone was expected to be dressed and ready to go by 7 a.m. for Mass. Victoria was curious about the Catholic faith and how the church celebrated its faith. She had every intention of drinking in the whole experience. She planned to tell her parents everything about the Catholic faith and how they worshiped.

Sunday morning Victoria was looking out the window and watching the sunrise. Victoria decided to explore the family home. There was a piano in the parlor covered in a beautiful gold scarf with pictures of the family sitting there proudly. The room was painted a soft eggshell white, with drapes of green and gold. The sofa and the chairs in the room were all overstuffed and comfortable. There was a massive fireplace made of marble with an oil painting of Grand Mere and Dr. Rogers hanging above. Across the foyer, there was the library for the family of doctors. There were medical books and law books, the desk was long enough to seat two people. The bookcases reached the ceiling there was a special ladder that rolled from side to side to enable you to get the books that were too high to reach. This room was done in soft gold, with matching tapestries and drapes of purple. There were pictures of family and people in politics.

She walked out the front door and stood on the porch overlooking the front yard, and the entrance to the main house. It was a humbling experience to see the accomplishments made by a single Negro family. This home and land were something special she could feel it all through her body. She decided to go down the steps and around to the back of the house. When she got down the steps, the first thing she ran into were the dogs. They never barked or growled; they came up to her to be patted. It was like they knew she brought them no harm. She and the dogs walked to the back of the house where the patio had been full of people and food from the night before.

The yard at the back of the house had deep green grass it sloped down to a small valley where Naomi and her husband built their home. It looked like a little cake, on a big green tablecloth from where she stood. There was a cobblestone path between the homes, used by Naomi and her husband as they walked back and forth to the main house. She walked around the yard and went halfway down the hill before she decided to go back. Victoria decided to go into the kitchen and start breakfast. She found all the ingredients she would need to make biscuits before the family came down for breakfast. Victoria made sixty biscuits.

The kitchen was huge with five coffee pots in the butler's pantry. There were four built-in ovens and a 12-burner stovetop, she could feel the love the kitchen had provided over the years. The walls were painted a bright yellow with kitchen pictures on the walls. Asher came into the kitchen, he was watching her, she was so thoughtful not only beautiful and sweet, to start breakfast for the family before his mother, sister and grandmother came downstairs. When he walked into the kitchen, she was putting the final touches on the biscuits. She was spreading butter on each one with a brush and putting them back in the oven to stay warm. Asher made himself a cup of coffee looking at Victoria with love in his eyes. Victoria was happy and pleased to start breakfast before Naomi, and Lady Katherine came into the kitchen. They gave Victoria hugs and blessings. Asher was amazed at how well she had handled herself to start breakfast. Everyone was waking up, they started coming downstairs to the kitchen to taste the hot biscuits.

Chapter 29

The Rogers family were dressed and ready for Mass. Victoria was able to see the different generations. Dr. Caleb Rogers had the look of an African King salt and pepper hair with warm brown skin and light brown eyes. Grand Mere was from New Orleans, Louisiana she was a creole with green eyes light caramel skin, and long cold black hair she combed into a bun that looked like a crown. Dr. Noah Rogers was Asher's father, a heavy-set man with dark-brown skin, salt and pepper hair, and brown eyes. Lady Katherine was Asher's mother, small in stature. Her skin was the color of coffee with heavy cream and her eyes were light brown with salt and pepper hair she wore shoulder length. Sister Naomi has light brown skin with light brown eyes. Last was Asher he stood 6-feet-tall sandy-brown hair, creamy skin like butter, and gray eyes. This family reflected their ancestors positively and beautifully. Lady Katherine came down the stairs.

"Everyone, it's time to leave for Mass and I don't plan for us to be late."

At that point, there were children, teenagers, and adults getting in their cars and driving to All Saints Catholic Church in Atlanta. Driving to the church was breathtaking to Victoria, the buildings in the city, people in their cars; this was a big city compared to Nashville.

When they arrived at their church there was a large circle that surrounded the church for letting people out at the door and the parking spaces. The church was made from Stone with a massive front door that was made of mahogany. There were marble floors and walls, the marble had been imported from Italy. The church was built by a wealthy sea captain. When he retired from the sea, he settled in Georgia with all his family and introduced the city to Catholicism. Walking into the vestibule there were small gold bowls of holly water which all dipped their fingers and then did the sign of the cross. Walking in the sanctuary, the floors were covered in red carpet which matched the cushions of the pews.

The middle aisle was not to be walked on out of respect. When the family found their way to their pew, they would genuflect before taking their seats; another sign of respect. The altar boys were lighting candles, and the choir was started to assemble. There was no choir processional as it was in the Baptist church at home. Once all was set, the processional started with the altar boy carrying the book of prayers followed by a cross that had a likeness to Jesus, and at the end was the Priest. Once he was settled and as the congregation stood, he said a short prayer and offered, "Peace be with You" the congregation replied, "And Also with You." There were people from the congregation who read different passages from the bible. During certain prayers, there was kneeling on padded benches.

After the homily, or sermon, was over, communion was offered. Wine and bread were served, this amazed Victoria. There was so much love in the room. When the Priest said show peace, everyone got up and shook hands and hugged saying, "Peace Be with You." Victoria was the visitor, and everyone made it a point to welcome her before they sat. The end of the service was the same going out the altar boys the book and at the end the Priest. There was so much going on Victoria could not keep up, but she knew this was special. Normally the family would stay for fellowship coffee and cake but since there was so many Rogers they decided to go home. On the ride back to the Rogers' home, Victoria closed her eyes and thought about a life with this amazing family and Asher as her husband, she said a short prayer, Father God, is Asher the man you sent me? Please give me a sign. At that moment, Asher took Victoria's hand into his and gave it a slight squeeze.

Everyone was back at the house the children and teenagers ran into the house to change from their church clothes into play clothes. The house was full of activity, the dogs were let in the house and were running up and down the stairs with the children.

Lady Katherine looked over the food in the kitchen, they were having leftovers from the party the night before. There were three turkeys, a ham, and desserts. The only thing missing was vegetables, Naomi was taking care of that. The family ate brunch, and everyone started to get sleepy. Victoria wanted a nap, but Asher told her they would be leaving at 3 p.m. going back to Nashville. Victoria felt torn, she wanted to go home but she also wanted to stay in Atlanta, this was the first time she did not want to go home after a trip. Victoria packed she placed her bags on the front porch. Asher pulled the car up to the grand staircase and parked.

The family started to stir, and they came to the door to say goodbye. Victoria hugged everyone goodbye and thanked them for inviting her into their home. The women of the family were waiting as the men said goodbye with handshakes and pats on the back.

Grand Mere pulled Victoria to the side and said, "You are a wonderful young lady. If you decide you love Asher, you have my blessing."

Victoria smiled, hugged the lady's saying goodbye to the men. Asher helped her into the car, they were on their way back to Nashville.

Chapter 30

The ride to Nashville was quiet not the same excitement as it was going to Atlanta. Asher never spoke unless he was asked a question and Victoria could feel the tension in the car. The hours passed like years now Victoria was ready to be at home with her family. Stopping for gas, Victoria got out to stretch her legs and asked Asher, "Did you enjoy your time in Atlanta? Do you want to move back once you have completed school?"

Asher looked at Victoria, a look she had never seen before, and replied, "Yes, I would love to be in Atlanta but to be a successful physician, sacrifices are sometimes made."

Victoria was shocked at his answer and the look, she felt she was responsible for keeping him away from his family.

The sun started to set as the couple drove over Mt. Eagle, Victoria knew this was the last miles to Nashville. The couple arrived in Nashville at 8 p.m., Jewel and Craig came out to greet their daughter. Asher helped Victoria out the car then helped her with her bags. Jewel could feel the tension in the air but did not want to ask any questions. Craig shook Asher's hand and welcomed him home. Craig could also feel the tension. The bags were taken into the house. Asher gave Victoria a quick hug, got into the car, and drove away. Victoria was exhausted mentally and physically; she was happy to be home. With school being out she would be able to get some much-needed rest.

The sun was shining bright, Victoria was awake she was not able to stay in bed, her mind was racing with memories from her trip. She could smell food from the kitchen. Victoria slipped on her robe and went down to see her mother.

Craig had gone to work so she would have her mother all to herself to try and make sense of the trip home and the interaction with Asher. Jewel was surprised to see Victoria was up and not sleeping in, but she decided not to ask any questions. When Victoria walked into the kitchen, Jewel hugged her and Victoria would not let go, she started to cry.

"Victoria, what is wrong? Was there a problem in Atlanta?"

The look in Victoria's eyes said it all, she was in pain, and it was caused by Asher. Victoria began to tell the story from the moment they drove off to Atlanta until their return, Jewel listened intensely. The women continued their talk over breakfast and Victoria knew she would need to pray for clarity. Jewel assured her daughter all would be revealed and to put it in God's hands. She hugged her mother and went to her room. She was on her knees praying when Jewel called, she had a phone call it was Asher. There was a lump in her throat when she answered the phone, she was expecting Asher to tell her he no longer wanted her to be in his life. Victoria answered.

"Hello Asher, how are you today?"

"I have been better, back to the hospital routine," he replied.

Victoria continued to listen. "I don't have any classes Thursday, will you let me take you to lunch?"

Victoria wanted to know what he was going to say, and she agreed to meet him for lunch.

Asher said, "I will come pick you up at 2 p.m. Thursday."

Victoria was curious and anxious. Victoria was dressed early she knew Asher would be on time and at 2 p.m., Asher was knocking on the door. Jewel answered the door, Asher gave her a hug, she called for Victoria to come downstairs. When Asher saw her, he smiled and looked at her the way he did in Atlanta. Victoria felt better but was not sure how their lunch date would go. Asher walked her to the car and took her hand as he helped her.

The restaurant was in the Jefferson Quarter, it was a beautiful day so the coupled decide to eat outside on the patio. Asher ordered for them, as the waitress walked away, he took Victoria's hand and said, "I'm sorry for the way I have treated you since we left Atlanta. I had so many emotions going I needed to sort them out. This was the first time I had brought a young lady to meet my family and it went so well it scared me. Everyone in my family loved you, you fit in so well and when Grand Mere told me I had her blessing, well, I was overwhelmed."

Victoria looked at Asher and thought, God has answered my prayers, Asher is the one!

The meal was over and as they drove back to Victoria's house the doubt had been replaced with hope. When Jewel saw her daughter, she was smiling and singing to herself, her prayers had been answered.

Victoria helped her mother with dinner so it would be hot and ready when Craig came home from work. During dinner, Victoria told them about the Rogers family, the Catholic church, and everything that happened at the anniversary party. Craig and Jewel were hanging on her every word. They could see how happy and completely in love she was with Asher and his family. The summer quickly went by, Asher and Victoria had become an official couple.

She would invite him to dinner and help him with his studies. When they were not together, they talked on the phone. Craig and Jewel watched as their little girl was now becoming a woman right before their eyes and it was good.

The end of summer was approaching, it was Labor Day weekend and time for the annual block party. It has always been a great time for everyone in the neighborhood; church members, family, and friends. Victoria and Jewel decided this year they were going to make desserts. Miss Tammy was baking fresh bread to go with the butter she made during winter. Asher and some of his medical school friends were also pitching in. It was because of Asher they were able to see another aspect of the city and get away from their studies.

The men were getting all the meats ready for the grill. Miss Tammy had a large yard that was used from time to time to roast a pig. Everyone was excited, the pig when it was removed from the pit. The pig was wrapped in cheese cloth, the skin was wiped down with special oils to help the pig come out crispy and brown. The pig was split down the middled and cleaned. The feet and head are not removed. Once the coals were put in the pit and turned red the pig was lowered into the pit. The pig is cooked in the pit for 20 hours, afterwards it was lifted and put on a wide rolling table. Once the pig was in position for the block party everyone gathered around to see the pig unwrapped. It was a beautiful golden brown the meat was soft. The pig was set on its split belly an apple was placed in his mouth. The sides of the tray were garnished with pineapple slices and green vegetables. Everyone who saw this process for the first time was fascinated. Craig was helping with the pig so once it was in place for the party he went into the house and asked Jewel for some sweet tea. She patted his head and arms with a cool cloth.

Asher knocked on the patio door and was invited inside. Craig and Jewel told Asher how the block party came to be. Asher listened but had other things on his mind. Craig asked,
"Asher, are you ok?"
"Yes sir," Asher replied.
"Is there anything we can do for you?"
Asher looked and asked, "Is Victoria around?"
This question alarmed Jewel, she did not want her daughter hearing any bad news. Asher asked them to sit down.

"Mr. and Mrs. Lee, I am sure you know I love your daughter with all my heart and soul. I know she loves me. Today, I want to ask her to marry me…if I have your permission."

Jewel immediately began crying, Craig stood up and shook Asher's hand.

"Yes, you have our permission to marry Victoria," he said.

Asher was so excited he dropped the ring box on the kitchen floor. When he picked it up, he opened a beautiful dark red box in it was Grand Mere's engagement ring. The ring was made in 14-carat gold, it had a 2-carat round center stone with a double ring guard in rubies as the wedding band. Asher had the blessing of his family in Atlanta and they were waiting for his phone call confirming he was engaged.

The sun started to set, and the block party was going well, everyone was dancing, talking, eating, and enjoying the cool evening air. Asher and Victoria were also enjoying the party. They had some of the pork and sampled all the food. They danced together and they laughed with the carefree ease of a child. Asher, Craig, and Jewel had talked about how he would propose.

He told them their song was "Only You," and when the record played, he planned to ask Victoria to dance. Everyone would dance around them and make a circle. When the song ends and all is quiet, he would ask Victoria to marry him, the plan was set. The tempo of the music changed as Asher helped Victoria to stand and walk to the street. Just as they stepped in the dance area, "Only You" started to play.

Asher said, "This is our song, let's dance."

Victoria took his hand they started to sway with the music. The other couples started to dance around, Asher and Victoria, by the time the music stopped they were standing in the middle of the circle.
Victoria never noticed, she had her head on Asher's chest and her eyes were closed. Asher stopped dancing and looked deeply into Victoria's eyes. He knelt on one knee, opened the ring box, and asked, "Victoria will you marry me?"

Victoria looked at Asher and the crowd, tears started to drop, she said, "Yes!"

Everyone let out a cheer, it was a joyous moment. Her parents congratulated the couple, everyone was hugging and kissing there was love in the air.
Everyone who saw the couple congratulated them shaking hands and hugs. Everyone wanted to see her engagement ring it was beautiful, the ring guard of Rubies was the wedding band, put back into the box until

the wedding.

Everything was put away Asher and Victoria walked into her family home to call the Rogers. They were just as excited the women started to talk about the engagement party, the wedding shower, the wedding, and the reception. Asher and Craig walked out the room so the women could talk and plan they were on the phone for two hours, it was beautiful. Everyone was happy and excited. The engagement was official, September 1, 1951.

Chapter 31

It was Sunday morning and everything looked fresh and bright to Victoria. She was now engaged to the love of her life; she had a ring. The day being Sunday, she thought she was going to be able to stay home and make wedding plans however, Jewel made it clear newly engaged or single she was expected to be in church and that was the end of that. Craig, Jewel, and Victoria dressed and walking out to the car when the phone rang. It was Asher on the phone he said he would meet the family at church. Asher did not want to go to Mass at the chapel on school grounds it was very small; it only held 15 people.

He decided it was time for him to see the Baptist religion, to see how family and friends reacted to worship. Asher walked over to the car to help Jewel and Victoria out of the car. Victoria was so happy to see him, she felt so proud knowing that this man was going to be her husband. They walked into the church, found a pew, and sat down. Asher saw there was no keeling benches.

Victoria laughed and said, "This is the way it is in a Baptist church. We don't kneel unless we were at the very front of the church asking for forgiveness or doing communion."

When he asked about communion, she said that it was only offered on the first Sunday.

"The Baptist church does not use real wine; they use grape juice and small crackers. This is how we worship the body and blood of Christ."

This was a strange question to ask because he had always been brought up with actual wine and bread. This was how the Baptist worship and he wanted to see everything and embrace it. Once everyone was in their seats, church service was going to start. At 9 a.m., the choir started marching down the aisle. They sang as they went to their positions in the choir stand behind the pulpit. Asher was amazed, he never saw 50 people in a choir. The female members all wore hats that matched their outfits. The deacons started to pray everyone sat down.

During prayer, the minister walked into the room and took his position at the pulpit. Reverend Ridley took over the prayer and the congregation said, "Amen." Reverend Ridley's wife sat on the front row watching as usual. Asher was interested in the young ladies wearing white, Victoria explained they were the ushers.

"They help if you need anything during service and also to keep order."

Asher then asked about the older women sitting in the front pews.

"They are the mothers and are some of the oldest women members. They belonged to the church they were married and we're now widows," Victoria said.

Asher looked around to see how everything worked. There was a stained-glass window close to where he and Victoria sat, it was cracked. The window was a picture of Jesus, the sun shined through the crack. Asher thought to himself, this is a sign that Jesus is shining his love down on his love for Victoria. It was time for Reverend Ridley to start his sermon. This morning he was preaching about fire and brimstone; he was adamant about people committing sins. When he said something the congregation agreed with, they said, "Amen." Church service started at 9 a.m. and it was now almost 12:30 in the afternoon. Asher could not understand why services were taking over two hours; Victoria laughed.

"This is what happens in a Baptist church service are long we try to cover every inch of the sermon and atmosphere of the church."

After the sermon, Revered Ridley asked the congregation if anyone wanted to come and join the church, that was another major aspect of the church. There were announcements about the sick and shut in, activities at the church and any business that was a concern, they also did a welcome. During the welcome, all visitors were asked to stand. Of course Asher was a visitor, when he stood up, he said his name and why he was there.

He told them he was engaged to Victoria, and everyone turned around clapped. Victoria was asked to stand next to him. It was a beautiful tribute; everyone was excited for Victoria; the congregation had known her all her life.

Before church was over, there was another song and prayer. The choir marched out, once they left, the remainder of the congregation also left. Asher was amazed at all the things he witnessed. Victoria loves her religion and that was reason enough for him to sit there and hold her hand.

Jewel and Craig took their car, Asher and Victoria drove back to the house in Nashville. When they arrived, Jewel went upstairs to change her clothes. Coming down the stairs, she announced she was going to start dinner. Craig and Asher sat on the back patio talking. When Jewel said dinner was ready, both men walked swiftly to the kitchen. They were excited and hungry. Jewel made fried chicken and Victoria helped her with the green beans, candied yams and their special cornbread. Asher and Craig washed their hands and sat waiting for the food to be placed on the table. Victoria placed the vegetables in bowls and cut the corn bread, that looked like cake, along with sweet tea. Asher remarked that he loves his mother's cooking, but it was nothing like this. Jewel made true southern food; it was the best. No one was talking because the food was so good.

The afternoon went well they discuss the wedding and what would be expected. I don't know what my mother, sister or my grandmother have planned. They're going to get together with Victoria in Atlanta.

Jewel looked up saying, "The bride is usually married in the city she is from."

Asher said, "Yes ma'am, that's usually how it happens but it was discussed about having different functions in different cities. Such as the engagement party my mother and grandmother want to host. Then there is shopping for the bridal dress, everyone has agreed on going to Chattanooga, to purchase the wedding dress."

Miss Tammy and others were making the bridesmaids dresses as their gift to the couple. The wedding shower will take place in Nashville because that is where Victoria's has her friends and family. The wedding and reception will also be in Nashville. The task of getting people in and out of Nashville and Atlanta would need help from God.

Victoria looked at her mother and said, "Momma, do you think this is going to be too much on you?"

Jewel assured them she could take care of things.

"What colors have you decided on for the wedding?" Asher asked Victoria.

Victoria looked at him and said she did not know. Asher made it clear the colors needed to be decided upon because the colors would be on display at the engagement party. The flowers, dresses, shoes the color scheme is needed to be decided. Jewel and Victoria looked at each other they had never planned a formal church wedding. Once the men stopped talking and finished dinner they decided to go back to the patio for dessert and coffee. While the men were on the patio, Jewel and Victoria talked.

"That was a good question, what are your colors?" Jewel asked.

Victoria told Jewel she wanted nothing but white flowers with touches of greenery decorating the church. She had not decided on the color for the bridesmaids' dresses. After talking with Miss Tammy, she would make her choice.

It was now about 8 p.m., Asher had spent the entire morning, and afternoon, with Victoria and her family. Asher had an early class, he would need to leave, everyone understood. Quick handshakes and a hug for Victoria. She walked him to the car where they kissed and held onto each other for dear life.

Asher would not see Victoria for another two days; he would see her after his rotation at the hospital ended. The final plans would be made at that time for the wedding.

"We can call my parents and let them know what's going on," Asher said.

The only thing Victoria realized she needed were dates and times to make some big decisions because a wedding takes time to plan and when you're doing one in two cities it's a lot more complex.

Jewel looked at her daughter saying, "No matter what happens, it is going to be a beautiful day because two loving souls are going to be united and that is what is most important."

Victoria smiled and shook her head, "Yes ma'am, I know. I'm so excited. I am so blessed I never thought in a million years that I would find someone to share my life who is as wonderful as Asher. I know he loves me his family loves me they are willing to accept me into their family no matter what my background is."

Jewel looked at her daughter patted her hand and said, "Time for bed, for all of us. We've had a very busy day, I'm going upstairs. Craig is going upstairs too but if you want to stay down here, that's fine but we're going to bed. I love you. I will see you in the morning."

"You have a wonderful man in Asher. He really loves you, I'm happy that you were blessed to find him. I love you. I'm going upstairs, I'll see you in the morning."

Victoria was left downstairs, she didn't turn on the lights, she sat in the dark and thought about her blessings. The people she had met, the good ones and the bad. She prayed for thankfulness when it came to her future in-laws and family; there are so many things that can cause strain on a marriage. That was not going to be the case for her and Asher. It suddenly dawned on Victoria that the family in Atlanta had not met her parents. Her family was small, she does have family and she wanted them to be included in any plans or functions that happen in Atlanta.

She sat back on the sofa and closed her eyes; she could see her wedding day as clear as if she were looking at a picture. She needed to go to bed because she had class in the morning starting at 7 a.m. Victoria went up the steps with a song in her heart and love for Asher. Once she got in her bedroom, she said an additional prayer just for him. She slipped into her nightgown and by the time her head touched the pillow, she fell straight to sleep. The alarms woke her at 6 a.m. Time to go back to school and continue making plans for her wedding. One thing that needed to happen was for her and Asher to decide on a wedding date. She would talk with Asher when they met in the cafeteria. Victoria thought of Asher on her way to class, feeling blessed with Asher's love.

Chapter 32

Victoria met Asher in the cafeteria between classes, she wanted to talk about setting a wedding date. He smiled when he saw her and came over to their table. They shared a sandwich.

"I have been thinking about a wedding date in Nashville. I was thinking June 7th because you and I will have graduated. That should give your family enough time to come to Nashville, it's only a four-hour drive," Victoria said.

"If you want June 7th, then that is the date," Asher replied.

Lunch time had passed, the couple had to get back to class. Victoria was so excited; she had an actual wedding date. She could not wait to get home to tell her mother they had decided on a wedding date. Asher was going home to call his family with the wedding date. Asher told Grand Mere the date would be June 7, 1952. The family was excited.

"I want to throw you and Victoria an engagement party," Grand Mere said. "I was thinking about April 19th, do you think that is a date that could work for you?"

Asher looked at his calendar, "I don't see any reason why that date won't work but before you put it down in your engagement book, I am going to Victoria's house later this evening and we will call you to make sure everything is on the right track."

When Craig picked up Victoria, she was very excited, she wanted to tell him they had set a wedding date but she wanted to tell her mother first. The minute she got home she ran to hug her and tell her that they had set June 7th as their wedding date. Jewel was so excited, the women hugged and danced around the kitchen. It was a great sense of relief because Jewel did not know exactly how far into the future the wedding would be.

Jewel was happy that Asher did not stand on ceremony and say he wanted to get his practice going before were married.

Victoria told her mother that the Rogers family would call tonight because they were trying to coordinate a date for an engagement party. Once that happens, they'd be all set for the first part of their wedding. Jewel and Victoria were excited they could hardly wait for 8 p.m.. Asher came over, he said that he was going to call his grandmother and then everyone can listen on the phone call.

Grand Mere answered the phone and explained to Victoria's family that she was going to have an engagement party for the couple in Atlanta. Victoria agreed to all the dates and time from Grand Mere. They talked about the color scheme; it was decided the color would be a soft blue.

"I want everything in the church to be white with hints of the blue and green from the flowers," Victoria said.

Grand Mere thought that was a beautiful combination, she would make sure the colors were on display at the engagement party. The date that was set for the engagement party, April 19th, it was a Saturday. Victoria walked Asher to his car, she was so excited, the engagement party and wedding dates were set. Victoria's dream of having a beautiful wedding and engagement party were going to come true.

"Momma, please book the wedding date for the church while I'm at school."

"Yes, my sweet girl. I will do that this morning. I love you have a good day at school."

Jewel called Reverend Ridley's wife, Gloria, and invited her to come to her house for lunch. Jewel had so much to share with the First Lady. When Gloria arrived, Jewel had everything set for a lunch that was special for a first lady. She made little sandwiches with the crusts cut off, salad, and chocolate cake for dessert. They had cups of tea instead of coffee as they talked about the future Mrs. Rogers. Gloria listened as Jewel told her what her daughter wanted. The church was to be decorated with white flowers with hints of blue, the color scheme, blue and white.

Gloria said she understood, that would be no problem she had several varieties of white flowers that had grown in her garden that she could use for Victoria's wedding. There were hydrangeas, lilies of the valley, magnolias, and primrose.

These flowers would make beautiful arrangements for the pews, the ceremony area and the pulpit. Jewel was relieved that the first lady would be happy to help and to supply all the white flowers.

"The date is June 7th," Jewel said.

Gloria wrote the date in her appointment book and assured Jewel that everyone would be happy to help with all the wedding plans.

Craig picked Victoria up from school, she was excited. She wanted to know if her mother was able to talk to the First Lady to make sure her date was available.

"I have not been home," he said.

Craig had no idea of any plans since he had been gone all day. Victoria was quiet as she thought about it, but she was so excited she could not hold it in. When she got home the first thing, she did was find Jewel and give her a hug. Jewel had great news about the flowers the date was booked at the church for the ceremony. The next big hurdle would be the food. Jewel knew how complex food can be for a wedding. You want enough food to feed the people, but you don't want to have too much that it goes to waste. Jewel made it clear to Victoria. She asked her how many people were going to be on the guest list.

Victoria looked at her saying, "Oh, I have not thought about the actual guests and how many to invite."

Jewel said, "I understand but you have got to give me a wedding guest list. How many bridesmaids are you going to have? How many groomsmen? These numbers need to be decided as soon as possible. There are people in Allen, I need to Invite Aunt Ivy of course, Mother Ida and Father."

Victoria looked around and she said, "You're right I need to get my emotions under control and take care of the business of planning this wedding so it will go off without a hitch. Momma I love you thank you for all your help and your wise advice. "I am going upstairs now and call Asher and talked to him about the groomsmen and how many people that he wanted to be attendance for the wedding."

Jewel looked at her daughter go up the steps and she went back into the kitchen to finish making dinner. Victoria called Asher to discuss the groomsmen and attendants. Asher said he wanted to have 4 groomsmen and his brother-in-law Richard will be the best man. Victoria needed four bridesmaids and the maid of honor would be Juanita.

The groomsmen are to wear black tuxedos with white flowers in the lapel, light blue bow ties and cummerbunds. She told him she wanted him to wear black tuxedo pants and a white dinner jacket with blue bow tie and blue cummerbund. Asher will ask some of his medical school friends to be ushers. Victoria did not want to have a big wedding party; she did not want a junior bridesmaid just two flower girls. Jewel was going to ask Miss Tammy if she will let her two granddaughters Michele and Lois be flower girls. All the preliminary plans for the wedding were going well. The bridesmaids' dresses were being made the blue was perfect. Mrs. Williams offered to make the wedding cake. The food for the wedding was going to be supplied by the Deacon Board. The neighbors and the church members have offered to help in any way possible. It brought Jewel to tears to know how much Victoria was loved by everyone who wanted to make her day perfect.

Chapter 33

Victoria and Asher were walking to the cafeteria. The holidays were coming and there were decisions to make. Victoria was going to Atlanta or stay in Nashville. Victoria mentioned the distance for the holidays, Thanksgiving was always special to her family. Asher asked if they would like to go to Atlanta and celebrate the holiday and meet his family. Victoria thought it may work out, but she will need to talk with her parents. Asher agreed and they continued their walk.

Craig picked Victoria up from school and could tell she had something on her mind.

"Are you ok? You are so quiet did something happen at school?" Victoria said, "no just thinking about plans for Thanksgiving."

When Victoria got home, she hugged her mother and went upstairs to change out of her uniform. When she came down the table was ready, Dinner was good as usual but there was no conversation about the day.

Jewel said. "Ok what is going on, why is everyone so quiet?"

Craig laughed "Talk with Victoria, she seems to have a question for us."

Asher's parents what me and your father to come to Atlanta for Thanksgiving. Asher, he wanted to know if you and daddy would want to go to Atlanta for Thanksgiving?" It is usually just us three so going to Atlanta would be festive and you will meet Asher's parents and extended family."

Jewel and Craig looked at each other, this was unexpected. "Well, is that something you would like to do?" Craig asked.

"Before we make a decision, Asher should talk with his family first."

Victoria agreed, she would talk with Asher to find out if they want to host her family for a major holiday.

Fall turned to Winter with snow and ice. Victoria had been busy with wedding plans, she wanted to ask Asher about Thanksgiving. Victoria and Asher were having lunch when she asked.

"Did you talk with your family about the holiday?"

Asher looked at her, "I thought everything was set for your family to travel to Atlanta."

Victoria was stunned, "When did you talk with your family?"

"I talked with them in October, I thought I had told you." Victoria started to laugh the back and forth to Atlanta is a little confusing, but I know my parents will enjoy the trip."

Asher smiled and pulled Victoria in for a big hug, he kissed her cheek. Craig picked up Victoria and the drive home, was light and fun.

"Momma, did you and daddy decide about Thanksgiving?"

"We are looking forward to the trip. Asher's grandmother called us in October to give us a formal invitation and let us know what to expect."

Victoria laughed, "I guess I'm the last one to know, I can't wait, you are going to love his family. And, we can show you around Atlanta."

The plan was to drive down in Asher's car leaving Nashville Wednesday afternoon. That will be three days of festivities and drive back Sunday. There were outfits to pack for Jewel and Victoria. Craig was going to pack light but that was not going to happen; Jewel packed for him, things were going as planned for Thanksgiving. Juanita came over to discuss the wedding shower. The date was May 10, 1952. All her friends from nursing school and high school were invited, not to mention the neighbors and church members. This was to be for the ladies but if men wanted to come, it was ok. Everyone knew Victoria would be living in Atlanta after the wedding.

The week of Thanksgiving was constant movement. Jewel promised to make four chocolate pies. It was cold outside so that would help keep the pies fresh. Jewel was going to pack them in special ice cream boxes she got from Craig. The trip started at 2 p.m., Wednesday. Asher called his parents to let them know they were on the road. The miles flew by as Victoria and Jewel looked out the window. Jewel was amazed at how things had changed from her move to Nashville when Victoria was a baby.

Craig and Asher were having "man talk" while Victoria and Jewel were napping. When they stopped for gas, everyone got out the car and stretched their legs. Asher announced there will only be an hour before they arrived at his parents. The sun had set the driveway lights leading to the house were bright and friendly. When they turned toward the house all the lights in the house were on. The grand stairway leading to the front door was lighted the family started to come outside to meet Asher and the Lee's. Jewel had never seen anything like it. She knew the Rogers family were prosperous, but she had no idea, it was like a fairy tale.

Grand Mere was out front welcoming the new family members. She hugged Jewel and welcomed Victoria back. The Roger's men were shaking hands with Craig and there were introductions. The bags were taken into the foyer. The parents were escorted to the formal dining area. The trip ended with the families meeting and praising God for their blessings, Asher and his new family arrived in Atlanta safely.

Chapter 34

Jewel walked, arms-locked, with Victoria. She was like a kid in a candy store, she had never seen such sights. The dinner table was set for a light dinner of salads, fruits, vegetables and breads. The tradition of the Rogers's was not to eat any meat Thanksgiving week until the actual day. That set well with Craig and Jewel, they had been on the road, and it was getting late, a simple meal was wonderful. Jewel asked one of the teenagers to fetch the deserts from the trunk. Once the family saw them, they were anxious to sample, Grand Mere said okay but there was to be only one slice per two people. No problem this was getting their stomachs ready for the rich food on Thanksgiving. After the meal was over, everyone retired to their bedrooms. Victoria was in the same pink bedroom she had on her last visit. Craig and Jewel were in the blue room. The room was painted blue all the linens and comforter were blue to compliment the walls.

The morning of Thanksgiving had finally arrived, dinner was set for 5 p.m. giving all out of town family members time to arrive. The Rogers men had a tradition on Thanksgiving morning, they would hunt for turkeys, quail and other small birds. The birds hunted that morning would be seasoned and stored for the winter months to come. Craig had never hunted but he was eager to learn, he didn't want to shoot the wrong thing so he decided he would help dress the birds and keep up with dogs.

Asher's father Dr. Noah Rogers talked with Craig, he thought Victoria was going to be an excellent member of the family. He continued to praise her loving ways and knew she reflected her family. Noah also said he and Jewel would be welcome anytime and that he hoped to get to Nashville.

The men continued to hunt, and Craig was showed the land and the story of how they became the owner of 1,000 acres of the richest and sought-after land in the state of Georgia. Craig smiled he was happy that Victoria's future was set with a loving giving family. He said a quick prayer, thanking God for this family and the love they showed Victoria and her family.

Back at the house there was organized chaos. The teenage boys were tasked to polish the silverware. The teenage girls were setting the main dining table with beautiful linen tablecloths and napkins. There were glasses and goblets for water, sweet tea and wine. This was new to the Lee family, wine with dinner. Jewel and Craig were looking forward to drinking wine while enjoying the beautiful meal that was being prepared.

The children's table was set in the kitchen overlooking the beautiful green backyard. Jewel was able to put her pies in a special place. Victoria and Jewel were helping with the vegetables and the baking of bread. Jewel enjoyed making bread, there were three small loafs that came out the oven first. The small loafs were cut and buttered for everyone to snack as the preparations continued. There was no Thanksgiving breakfast the men left the house early to hunt and the women got started on dinner. Along with the breads were cheeses and fruit placed in the Butler's Pantry. Naomi was singing, Jewel recognized the tune, they sang as the different foods were prepared. Victoria was happy to see how everyone was warm and loving to her parents. Victoria was truly in love with her new family. She started to hum, thanking God for Asher and his family.

More relatives started to arrive and were greeted by Grand Mere, she coordinated the sleeping arrangements, luggage and making all feel welcome. Doing this and keeping an eye on the Thanksgiving preparations, she was an elegant site to behold. The final touch, Grand Mere, put place cards next to the glassware.

While the food was set to rest the ladies went upstairs to freshen up and change clothes. Once Grand Mere was dressed ready or not you were expected to be in your place. Dinner was announced by Dr. Caleb, and everyone went into the dining room. The different foods were placed on the table. There were two, 15-pound turkeys and two hams, breads, butter, vegetables and fruit. Dr. Caleb blessed the food, before the meal started everyone was asked to say what they were thankful for. There were those who were thankful for the family, the bounty that had been given. The Rogers men said they were thankful for their wives. Asher said he was thankful for Victoria, and she said the same of him. Craig and Jewel were thankful for the Rogers family and how they were welcomed into their home but mostly for their son. Some tears dropped the food was passed. Jewel and Victoria were helping clear the table for dessert and coffee. The women giggled they had enjoyed the wine. After desert the men retired to the study for brandy and cigars. This was new to Craig, he enjoyed everything about the Rogers traditions. The ladies of the house retired to the back patio some with desert others with tea. The sun had gone down. The lights for the patio were turned on, they looked like twinkling stars. Craig made a fire in the fire pit for the ladies to enjoy and fight off the chill of the evening. They enjoyed the fire as it burned bright and warm.

Chapter 35

Friday after Thanksgiving was a very quiet day no one was in a hurry to do anything, it meant even the Rogers men slept in. When the men came down for their breakfast, they could see it was not ready they decided to get coffee and go onto the back patio. Dr. Caleb was showing Craig the back side of the property since it was dark when they arrived. Craig listened when he said all the children in the family had their homes built and lived on the property.

Craig thought if Asher returns to Atlanta to practice medicine that meant he and Jewel would be alone with Victoria in Nashville; he knew his thoughts were selfish. That was not what he wanted but he realized Victoria would have her own family and would follow her husband.

They were still talking about the hunting trip on yesterday, the men thought Craig fit in even though he did not shoot a rifle. Naomi and Jewel met in the kitchen to get breakfast started it was going to be a hearty breakfast because that was going to be the only meal of the day that was cooked until dinner. Dinner was going to be served at 8 p.m. Friday night. Victoria awakened and realized that she was back in her favorite pink bedroom at the Rogers home.

She knew her mother was downstairs; she could hear her singing. That meant she was the only one downstairs in the kitchen. Grand Mere and the other ladies in the family had not come downstairs. The house was overrun with cousins and aunts and uncles from New York, Washington DC, Virginia and California. All the men in the Roger's family had degrees from some of the most prestigious Negro Universities in the country.

The heart of the family was Grand Mere her husband Dr. Caleb Rogers, Lady Katherine and her husband Dr. Noah Rogers. Naomi being a girl was not in succession for the land to build a home. The land she had in the valley was given to her by Grand Mere. She wanted her only granddaughter to be close and if Grand Mere wanted to interrupt the line, then it was interrupted no questions.

Seeing all the different license plates, the Rogers had extended family all over the country. Victoria jumped up got a shower dressed and was ready to meet the day. On her way down the steps, she was tripped by the dogs, everybody thought that was such a funny scene because she just laid there, and the dogs licked her trying to get her up it was cute.

Victoria walked into the kitchen she realized that she could help get breakfast together for everyone and so instead of trying to cook she decided she was going to make sure she set the table and had the food arranged beautifully with juice glasses and goblets for water. She changed the linen tablecloth from the night before. Breakfast was ready and everyone was called to eat, the formal announcement was only for dinner, if you missed the breakfast call it was possible to miss breakfast al together.

The young people's table was set but as usual the boys were outside, and some did miss breakfast. In the meantime, those who missed the hot breakfast were served oatmeal and fruit, they missed the biscuits, ham, bacon, eggs and home fries; Grand Mere was very serious about order in her house.

The day started to turn into afternoon and the menus were reviewed because there were other family members expected. Grand Mere put that aside and called Jewel and Victoria to bring the wedding plans and meet her at the table overlooking the back garden. Victoria was excited to talk about the wedding, Jewel was still uneasy about the Rogers, she felt they were taking her daughter's choice away. She knew they were good people, but Jewel was her only child. All the dress designs and colors were on display. Grand Mere went over the date for the engagement party.

"I have a guest list of 200. Victoria," she asked, "how many of people do you have set for the engagement party?"

Victoria started to think how many people she knew would be able to come to Atlanta. "I think I have 50 people, but I will get a final head count when I'm back home."

The engagement party was set for April 19, 1952, in Atlanta this date was set in stone. The wedding shower was confirmed for May 10, 1952, in Nashville; wedding date, June 7, 1952.

"I need a head count for your family for the wedding," Jewel said.

Grand Mere said, "75, maybe one hundred. I will get a final head count after the holidays."

The date and number of attendees were written in Grand Mere's engagement book, there was no changing once it was written down. These dates were discussed and again the dates were set in stone.

"Tomorrow is Saturday, since everyone is here in one place, it would be a perfect time to shop for the wedding dress, any objections?" Grand Mere asked. There were none. "The meeting is over we need to get busy on tonight's dinner."

Jewel was again feeling like her daughter was being pushed and she felt they had no say so in her wedding. Jewel asked Victoria to show her the back of the property.

They walked outside Jewel asked, "Tell me the truth, are the Rogers taking away your choice when it comes to the wedding?"

Victoria looked at her mother, "No momma, they have been very kind with everything. I know what you mean but I want Asher to be proud of the wedding in Nashville."

Jewel looked at Victoria, all she could see was the big-eyed little girl asking if everything was ok after the tornado. Jewel kissed Victoria and said, "it's all for you, it will be a beautiful here in Atlanta and Nashville."

Victoria was called by Asher to meet some of the new family members that had arrived. Jewel watched her little girl walk away with tears in her eyes. The men were leaving the study, Craig noticed Jewel was alone on the patio. When he walked up behind her, she turned and buried her face in his chest. He knew why she cried; she did not need to say a word. Friday dinner was, as usual, was beautiful everyone enjoyed the meal. The men disappeared and the women cleaned. Grand Mere came into the kitchen for final inspection.

"Ladies, tomorrow be ready to leave for the wedding gown search at 9 a.m. Breakfast will be served at 7 a.m. It's 11 p.m., everyone off to bed."

There were good night kisses and hugs everyone was ready for bedtime it had been a long day. No one mentioned the men, but the ladies knew they would appear at 7 a.m. Just as predicted the men lumbered to the kitchen to have breakfast. The ladies were all set to go wedding dress shopping. It was Grand Mere, Lady Katherine, Naomi, Jewel and Victoria. They talked about driving to Chattanooga to look for a wedding dress, but it was decided to start in Atlanta. The shops were in downtown Atlanta. The car passed a shop, Victoria saw a beautiful dress in the window. She pointed it out when they passed. The ladies went inside, and everyone looked at the dress in the window. Victoria looked at the dress and the expression on her face said it all, the clerk took the dress from the window. Victoria's put the dress on, and the clerk told her it was a perfect fit. The dress was white with elbow sleeves covered in pearls. The dress fell from the waist to the floor in satin and lace into a free fall. When Victoria walked out of the dressing room she looked like a beautiful princess. The older ladies looked at the dress and agreed this was the one. The price was $500, Victoria hung her head, she knew the dress was out of her price range, she welled up, but she refused to let Jewel see she disappointment. Victoria returned to the dressing room she tried other dresses but only the first one made her feel special. Victoria decided to go to another store, everyone agreed. The women went to four different stores, but none were as special as the dress in the window. The stores closed at 5 p.m. it was decided to go home have dinner and talk. Victoria was sad and Jewel knew they could not afford a $500 wedding dress. The men were out front when the car pulled up, Grand Mere got out first and went to her husband to talk.

Jewel and Victoria went upstairs, Jewel did understand how she was feeling. The evening meal was only the immediate family. The extra family members left that afternoon to go home and rest for Monday's workday. Jewel and Victoria went upstairs to pack they were leaving Sunday after Mass. Sunday morning after a light breakfast, everyone drove to 8 a.m. Mass. Craig and Jewel were anxious about going to Mass but were reassured by Victoria it was a beautiful service. At the end of the service Craig and Jewel saw the beauty of the Catholic Faith, they could feel how special the service and traditions were.

Everyone went back to the main house for brunch and to send the little family back to Nashville. Victoria was ready to go home, she had such a heavy heart. Asher and Craig loaded the car with the luggage. Grand Mere called everyone together for the farewell. There were hugs, kissing and handshakes. They were all in the study, Grand Mere asked.

"Victoria, do you have everything packed?"

"Yes," she said.

"I think you are missing one last piece of clothing."

Grand Mere pulled a large box from behind the door and gave it to Victoria. When she saw the box, she started to cry, tears of joy. Opening the box, it was the wedding dress she saw in the window. Jewel told her it was too generous, and she could not accept the dress.

"This dress is a gift from Naomi, accept the gift."

All the ladies hugged and cried the men left the room and went out to the car.

"How can I accept something so lovely?" Victoria asked. Naomi said, "If I had a daughter, I would want her to have the dress of her dreams, so this is for you, I look forward to seeing you walk down the aisle in June."

The women hugged and the dress was packed for Nashville. Asher gently placed the dress in the car along with the small family. Victoria leaned over on her momma and fell asleep. The ride to Nashville was quiet everyone was reflecting on the holiday weekend.

Chapter 36

The family returned to Nashville, once the car was unloaded Asher said, "I'm going home, I'm tired. I love you."

Victoria agreed, she kissed Asher goodbye. Victoria was in her room looking at her wedding dress, she was so happy and proud. Asher was going to be surprised when he sees her walk down the aisle. Jewel and Craig watched their daughter with her dress, they were happy she got the dress of her dreams but sad they could not afford the dress. Victoria saw them.

"Momma, please don't be sad about this dress! You know you have taken care of me all my life. Over the years you have spent more than $500 on me, and this dress is just a very small part of raising me. Yes, this dress is special, but not nearly as special as you've been to me. While I love this dress, I love you more! If this dress makes you feel uncomfortable, I will send it back. I will never do anything to jeopardize our love or make it seem like I'm ungrateful."

Jewel hugged her daughter, Craig hugged them both. It was going to be ok; their love and family bond was stronger than a $500 dress.

December was a special month with Christmas and New Year's. There was no big dinner planned with family and friends this year. It seemed everyone had made plans to leave town for Christmas.

Victoria realized with having family out of town, all the holidays and special occasions would be spent traveling. Asher went to Atlanta, he would be back so he and Victoria could see in the New Year together. Christmas break from school started December 21st until the first Monday after New Year's. Asher would be home Friday the 20th, Victoria really missed him. She talked with him on the phone, but it was not the same. Asher was finally home, and Victoria wanted to spend as much time as possible with him. He had a small apartment close to the medical school and his roommate went home for Christmas he would not return until after the 1st for class. Asher and Victoria would have the place to themselves.

Victoria decided to stay in and cook for Asher on New Year's Eve versus going out. When Victoria arrived, Asher had a fire going and candles around the apartment, it was perfect. Victoria had the traditional food, greens, black eyed peas, mashed potatoes and cornbread. She did not cook, at Asher's apartment she brought the food from home, he could thank her momma. After dinner the couple fell asleep on the sofa. It was10 minutes to midnight, Asher opened a bottle of champagne to toast the new year, at midnight they toasted and had a long deep kiss. During the kiss Asher ran his hand down the side of Victoria's dress and cupped her breast in his hand. Victoria jumped this was the first time they been alone, she really had no idea how to react. When he started to caress her legs and thigh she got up from the sofa.

Asher asked, "What's wrong?"

Victoria said to him, "We have never been alone like this. I know we are engaged but sex is for the marriage bed."

Asher looked puzzled, he asked, "Have you never done anything sexual?"

Victoria shook her head no. Asher got up from the sofa and pulled Victoria close and asked, "Are you still a virgin?"

Victoria said, "Yes, I don't want to disappoint you, but I'm not sure how to react to you. You will need to teach me everything."

Asher looked at this beautiful innocent girl, kissed her forehead and pulled her close.

"You are the woman I want and love, its only five months until the wedding and I will keep my emotions under control."

They kissed, sat on the sofa, talked, and fell asleep in each other's arms. Asher was up later that morning, He made toast and coffee for Victoria, they talked and ate the small breakfast.

"I better get you home."

"Yes," Victoria said, "I'm sure my parents are concerned I won't call them, I'll just go home."

Asher dropped Victoria at her house and drove back to his apartment. Jewel was in the kitchen having coffee with Craig, they had a look on their faces she had never seen before.

"Well, it's good you were able to find your way home," Craig said.

Her mother just looked on waiting to hear her explanation as to where she had been all night.

Victoria smiled, "Momma, daddy, I spent the night with Asher. We talked about the wedding and our life together. Nothing happened. But for whatever reason, Asher did not know I was a virgin. We kissed and ate the food momma made."

Craig looked on, "Are you sure nothing happened?"

"Yes, we're waiting until our wedding night," said Victoria.

Jewel got up from the table and hugged her daughter, she was relieved in so many ways. She did not want her to be hurt like she was.

The days started to fly by, it was time for the engagement party. Asher drove to Atlanta with Victoria and her parents. There was a band with a singer. The engagement party was an elegant affair everyone was dressed in formal wear and Victoria's colors were on display. The tables were covered in white linen with blue accent tablecloth, blue bows on the white chairs. Once the party got started Asher and Victoria entered, everyone stood and clapped.

Craig and Jewel watched as their little girl stepped into womanhood, Jewel felt confident her daughter was going to have a wonderful life with this family. The couple had their first dance to their song, Only You. Once the song ended it was ok for the other guests to dance. The food was served in courses just as it had been at the anniversary party. The champagne flowed everyone ate and fun was had by all. The gift table was full and continued to grow It was a wonderful evening. Craig and Jewel sat watching the party and the people. When the clock struck midnight, the band said goodnight, and people started to leave. Asher and Victoria went to the study closed the door to enjoy some quiet time. Another beautiful event coordinated and planned by Grand Mere.

Sunday everyone was tired, and they missed 8 a.m. Mass. Lady Katherine rolled over and looked at the clock it was 9 a.m., she knew Grand Mere would be upset she missed Mass, but to her surprise she was in the kitchen drinking coffee with some deserts left from the party.

"Good morning. We missed Mass, are you upset?" Lady Katherine asked.

"Actually, I'm not. I think everyone needed the extra rest."

The kitchen became busy as the family came downstairs and was pulling food from the refrigerator no formal meal.

Asher said, "We are leaving at 2 p.m., everyone get packed so we can get to Nashville before it gets dark."

Everyone agreed the car was packed, and off to Nashville they went.

Chapter 37

The day of the wedding shower had come, May 10, 1952. Victoria was more excited than normal because after today, she would only have four weeks before she walked down the aisle. Everything was falling into place, the bridesmaids' dresses are set for their final fittings next week, the reception tables chairs, linens, glassware and silverware were ordered and would be delivered Friday, June 6th. The reception was going to be on the church lawn under a large tent, the round tables sat ten people, the guest list had grown RSVPs were coming in every day. She received a yes to the wedding from Aunt Ivy, Mother Ida and Father. The deacons were doing the food and music. They were also going to act as waiters during the reception. They were to wear cut away jackets and white gloves. Hotel reservations were made for out-of-town family. The Sr. Rogers had friends in the area they were coming to the wedding they offered their homes for guests and family.

  The family had arrived at 1:30 p.m.. The shower was to be held at the church in the downstairs meeting room which could hold 100 people, it was an overflow. It was set to start at 2 p.m.. People were arriving and by 2:30, the room was packed with children and adults.

  The food tables were set up in the hallway buffet style. Victoria and her mother were sitting surrounded by gifts. Everyone had eaten and were enjoying sweet tea when Victoria started to open her gifts. The community was generous with their love. She received, linens, glass wear, silverware and china. There were also pot, pans, and an Electrolux vacuum cleaner. Serving platters, matching bowels, small appliances; hand mixer and coffee pot. The first of June is harvest time, many of her friends would be in the field. These friends and family brought her gifts to the shower. Victoria and Jewel thanked everyone for the gifts and love.

  When the shower was over, there were friends who offered to help take the gifts to Victoria's home. The house was filled with gifts of all shapes and size. Craig tried to help organize them, but the women had a different idea, so he just went out back and sat on the patio. Jewel was making the wedding cake, Victoria requested a white cake with white icing blue flowers it was going to be four tiers, also there was the groom's cake. Victoria wanted it to be the shape of a doctor's bag. Jewel had been experimenting with the look of the cake which was going to be chocolate.

With all the wedding plans under control Victoria started to think about graduation for herself and Asher.

The Rogers were going to be in Nashville for Asher's graduation. Victoria's graduation from Nursing School was scheduled for May 30, 1952. The medical school graduation was June 6th the day before the wedding, which was perfect, the Rogers family would be in town for the graduation and the wedding was the next day.

Victoria graduated, she was the Valedictorian, her speech was perfect for the day. Asher, her family and friends were there to cheer for her after the speech and when she received her diploma.

Afterwards everyone went back to Victoria's home for refreshments. Jewel and Craig were so proud of their daughter.

They watched as she danced with Asher. They had wonderful friends; the family was blessed. Jewel offered sandwiches and sweet tea to the couple and friends who were dropping by the house. Those who dropped gifts and to congratulate the couple, love was everywhere. The couple wanted some alone time, so they went to Asher's apartment.

Jewel and Craig said good night to the last few people that stopped to see the couple. Craig sat on the sofa and Jewel joined him, curling up in his lap.

"It has been a wonderful day, next week our little girl will be getting married, time flies. Asher will graduate next week; our children are going to have a blessed life together," Craig said.

"Yes, they will," Jewel said as she fell asleep in his arms.

Graduation for Asher was special, his parents and grandparents were in attendance. The family and friends watched as he walked across the stage and received his diploma. The Rogers family cheered and clapped. After graduation everyone wanted to have dinner. Victoria had last minute things to take care of for the wedding, she and Juanita left the graduation hall.

She kissed Asher and said, "This time tomorrow we will be man and wife."

He smiled and hugged her goodbye. The girls left to complete the final touches decorating the church. The bridesmaid dresses were ready and hanging at Miss Tammy's house to be picked up. Both cakes were ready the wedding cake looked like a picture from a magazine. The icing was white, the inside was blue, with blue roses cascading down one side. The groom's cake also turned out to be perfect.

The First Lady came by to drop off Victoria's bouquet. It was done in Magnolia flowers it was pulled together tight to make a full circle wrapped in blue silk. It was placed in the refrigerator. She and Jewel went to the church to do some decorating while Victoria rested. The candles were placed, and the pews were decorated with the same flowers as her bouquet. The alter was also decorated with candles, there were white flowers on the archway the couple would stand under; there was greenery and blue silk on the arch that matched the bridesmaids' dresses.

Today was her wedding day, the processional was to start at 5 p.m.. Victoria was a ball of nerves. The photographer came to the house to take before pictures, Jewel gave him directions on what pictures to take. Grand Mere arrived offering her help. Jewel asked her to talk with Victoria and help her into her dress. Jewel also came into Victoria's room; she had the traditional gifts for a bride. There was the something old, a handkerchief from Big Momma she had kept after the tornado. Something new was her dress, something borrowed was a pearl necklace from Lady Katherine. The blue was the silk woven into her bouquet. Victoria was dressed, her veil was woven into her hair. The veil was pulled down as she walked down the aisle, Asher was to pull it up for the kiss.

Craig drove the ladies to the church; they could see the tent and hear the music. The bridesmaids and the groomsmen were lined up at the front door for the procession down the aisle. "Ava Maria" started to play, which was the signal to start the wedding processional. The flower girls walked the aisle dropping white rose petals. The groomsmen and bridesmaids walked down the aisle two-by-two.

The best man had Victoria's wedding ring, Juanita was holding Asher's ring which was two toned in white and yellow gold with a wheat design. "Ava Maria" continued to be played, Victoria stepped into the church doorway she could hear the guests say how beautiful she was walking down the aisle. She looked down at her dress and smiled she wanted to be beautiful for Asher.

Aunt Ivy, Mother Ida and Father looked at Victoria come down the aisle. Mother Ida cried; Father put his arm around her shoulder. He thought she was going to pull away instead she leaned back as the tears flowed. Mother Ida and Father were in a better place. Time and prayer were healing their hearts and their marriage. Craig walked Victoria down the aisle she leaned on him for support, she was so nervous. Asher looked at Victoria, he wiped tears from his eyes, she was beautiful. She was all his, his love and soon his wife.

Reverend Ridley smiled and asked, "Who gives this woman to be married?"

Craig and Jewel said, "We do!"

Victoria gave her bouquet to Juanita, she and Asher held hands turning to face Reverend Ridley.

"The couple have written their vows."

The couple turned to face each other as they said their vows.

"Asher, today I marry my best friend. I promise to love and honor you all the days of our lives together. I have found the other half of my soul, the love of my life. I promise to be faithful and true. I will always support you I will lift you up. I love you."

"Now you Asher," said the Reverend.

"Victoria, when I look into your eyes, I see our unborn babies. I never thought I would meet my soul mate but today you stand before me. I promise to care for you and our future family. I love you; I want to be with you until God calls us home."

The ceremony continued.

"Wedding rings represent the unbreakable bond of a lifelong love a commitment between a man and a woman with the exchange of rings concreted by God.

Victoria, do you take this ring from Asher, to be his wedded wife? To have and hold, for better or worse, in sickness and in health?"

"I do," said Victoria.

Asher placed the ruby ring on her finger.

"Asher, do you take this ring from Victoria? To be her wedded husband? To have and to hold, for better or worse, in sickness and in health?"

"I do," Asher said, as Victoria placed the ring on his finger.

"If there are no objections, I now pronounce you man and wife. Asher, you may kiss your wife."

Asher lifted Victoria's veil and gave her a sweet kiss on the lips. The couple walked out the church into the evening mist, followed by the wedding party. The First Lady played piano as the guests left the church and started to the reception tent. There were two photographers taking pictures of the wedding party, family and friends. The first dance was to their song, "Only You." The reception was beautiful under the white tent lit with dozens of candles. Once dinner served there were toasts to the couple. Asher's grandfather stood up to toast the couple.

"This has been a wonderful night; I am so proud of my grandson and his new wife. The Rogers have a tradition, of giving land to the male heir and his new wife to build a home in Atlanta. Asher and Victoria, we gift you five acres of Rogers land."

Asher stood up, hugged his grandfather and shook his hand. Everyone clapped and gave another toast as bottles of champagne were opened.

"I am the patriarch of this family. I want happiness and prosperity for my immediate and extended family," Dr. Caleb Rogers said. "Asher will return to Atlanta to join the family practice. Craig and Jewel are losing their only daughter. We don't want Victoria to miss her family, her feelings are very important to us. I will bestow to our new extended family, Craig and Jewel, two acres of Rogers land to build their future home. Victoria is a beautiful soul who loves my grandson. Family is the most important aspect of one's life."

Everyone at the reception praised God and the Rogers family. Craig and Jewel were overwhelmed, they both cried tears of joy. The tears were flowing between Victoria, Jewel and Mother Ida.

"Jewel, please forgive me for the way I treated you. Leaving you as an infant, and then putting you in an awful position when I brought you to Allen," Mother Ida said. "I love you with all my heart. Will you call me momma, and not Mother Ida? Victoria, will you call me grandma?"

Jewel and Victoria looked at each and shook their heads yes.

The families have been brought together in love, after years of hurt, pain and sorrow. The families hugged and cried together. Aunt Ivy cried as she hugged Jewel and Victoria. The most important men and women in Victoria's life were there to see her happily married to a wonderful man.

The reception continued, Victoria threw her bouquet, it was caught by Juanita. The wedding cake was cut, Victoria fed a slice to her new husband. The groom's cake was cut and a slice was fed to Victoria by her new husband.

Asher and Victoria left the reception to change clothes for their getaway. They drove off in a blue Jaguar. Their wedding night was being spent in a hotel in the Jefferson quarter. They were headed to Niagara Falls for a weeklong honeymoon.

Jewel and Craig were happy, their daughter was married to a wonderful man. Today the Lee family gained a new family and a new home. Victoria had her fairytale wedding, she was destined for a beautiful life, they all were blessed.

The ancestors smiled upon the couple as they drove away from the church, it was a good day.

About the Author

My name is Teresa E. Banks, I am the last of my bloodline. I retired from the insurance industry; I am also a Navy Veteran. Thinking about my grandmother, the stories she told me as a child, started to form in my mind's eye. *A Love Sublime* was born.

My grandmother and my great-grandmother were the *Keepers of Light,* our ancestors' stories. These women told stories of our heritage; we are descendants of Royalty. My ancestors were abducted from Africa our homeland. Stripped of all humanity, forced into slavery, to endure inhumane treatment and death. We are a strong people connected to Spirit. I look to the heavens, at the stars, knowing I am looking at the same sky as my ancestors. These stories have given me peace, resolve and a connection to the Mother Land. This book was written for my ancestors, to keep our stories alive beyond the 21st Century.

I do not want these stories to end with me. I share my stories with those who may have lost a connection to their ancestors. I hope these stores help them find peace, as these stories have given me peace over my lifetime.

Got an idea for a book? Contact Curry Brothers Publishing, LLC. We are not satisfied until your publishing dreams come true. We specialize in all genres of books, especially religion, self-help, leadership, family history, poetry, and children's literature. There is an African Proverb that confirms, "When an elder dies, a library closes." Be careful who tells your family history. Our staff will navigate you through the entire publishing process, and we take pride in going the extra mile in meeting your publishing goals.

Improving the world one book
at a time!

Curry Brothers Publishing, LLC
PO Box 247
Haymarket, VA 20168
(719) 466-7518 & (615) 347-9124
Visit us at www.currybrotherspublishing.com

www.ingramcontent.com/pod-product-compliance
Lightning Source LLC
Chambersburg PA
CBHW050413120526
44590CB00015B/1946